JACK BERRY'S GUIDE TO MICHIGAN GOLF

by Jack Berry
Golf Writer, The Detroit News

Momentum Books Ltd.
Ann Arbor, Michigan

COPYRIGHT © 1991 by Momentum Books Ltd.

All rights reserved. No part of this book may be used or reproduced in any manner whatsoever without prior written permission of the publisher, except in the case of brief quotations embodied in critical articles and reviews.

Manufactured in the United States of America

1993 1992 1991   6 5 4 3 2 1

Momentum Books Ltd.
210 Collingwood, Suite 106
Ann Arbor, Michigan 48103

ISBN 1-879094-02-9

CONTENTS

From the Publisher	vii
Acknowledgements	ix
Preface	xi
How to Use This Guide	xv

COURSES
Wayne County	3
Oakland County	11
Macomb & St. Clair Counties	21
Washtenaw, Livingston & Monroe Counties	29
South Central Michigan	37
Southwest Michigan	45
Middle Michigan East	57
Middle Michigan West	67
Northeast Michigan	81
Northwest Michigan	91
Upper Peninsula	103

INDEXES AND OTHER INFORMATION
The Scoop on Slope	111
Designs on Golf	113
Why Did They Name It?	123
Hot Dogs With a View	125
Best Views From the Course	126
Trees, Trees and More Trees	127
Golf Schools	128
Tournament Courses	130
Trips	132
Shops	133
Counties & Regions	141
Alphabetical List of Public Courses	143

Jack Berry's
Guide To Michigan Golf

FROM THE PUBLISHER

Jack Berry has the perfect credentials to write the definitive guide to Michigan public golf courses.

Berry is a past president of the National Golf Writer's Association. He is now secretary-treasurer of that organization. And he is regarded nationwide by his peers, by the game's leading golfers, architects, and course operators for his integrity, insight, and knowledge of the game.

But that alone would not qualify Berry for this task. That took a career that has been a lifetime in the building. That took the deep understanding of the game that can come to someone who has travelled literally millions of miles covering golf around the world. It took a reporter's uncanny sense of the story and a well-honed gift of writing talent to tell that story. And certainly it took a comprehensive and intimate knowledge of the Michigan golf scene.

When you look at all those considerations, it is quickly clear that the task of writing the authoritative, user-friendly guide to Michigan's public golf courses is a task tailor-made for one person — Jack Berry.

So here it is. In the same sure easy style that has earned Berry praise from every quarter. Use Berry's Guide as you plan your next round in the next county over, as you plot a golfing vacation tour in new territory, as you seek a golf equipment or repair shop, a teacher or a golf school or camp from the many helpful lists and categories Berry has compiled in the back of the book.

And let Jack or us have your comments and thoughts so they can be reflected in next year's edition. Because that's one thing Jack Berry has taught us about golf in Michigan — there is always something new just a short iron shot over the horizon.

Bill Haney
June, 1991

ACKNOWLEDGEMENTS

For many years now I've written in *The Detroit News* about Michigan having more public golf courses than any state in the union including the Sun Belt and the Cactus Corridor. Writing it and enumerating them one by one are completely different matters, however.

I've been fortunate in more than 30 years of covering golf in Michigan to meet a lot of nice people and I called on many of them for assistance in this project.

My thanks to, in alphabetical order, Bob Bernstein of the Flint Junior District Golf Association; Lin Buck of Spalding Golf; Jim Buckley of the *Saginaw News;* Jim Caras of the University of Michigan; Vic Chiasson of the Wayne County Parks and Recreation Department; Nick Edson of the *Traverse City Record Eagle;* Mark Gilmore, PGA professional at Marquette Country Club; Chet Jawor of Jawor's Gratiot Golf; Richard Knoll of the Upper Peninsula Golf Association; Steve Kusisto, PGA professional at Lenawee Country Club; Jim Lajoie of the *Marquette Mining Journal;* Joe Luyckx of the Golf Association of Michigan; Bill McDonald, president of the Michigan Publinx Golf Association; Terry Moore, editor of the *Michigan Golfer;* Dave Richards of Golf Marketing Services, Ralph Richards of the Oakland County Parks and Recreation Department; Jim Roschek, PGA professional at Milham Park in Kalamazoo; Ken Smelko of the *Bad Axe Tribune;* Fred Stabley Jr. of Central Michigan University; John Vande Heeden of the *Benton Harbor Herald-Palladium;* Brent Veenstra, PGA professional at Hillsdale Country Club; and Wally Wheeler of Cheboygan Country Club.

PREFACE

Michigan has more public golf courses than any state in the union. That flat statement, based on National Golf Foundation statistics, always is good for a double take by my Sunbelt colleagues. Not only does Michigan have more public courses, it is one of only seven states with 1 million golfers. Not bad for a state of 9.2 million citizens with uncertain springs, too-short summers and autumns and too-long winters.

Obviously, Michiganians like to play golf and that's why, at the suggestion of Momentum Books publisher Bill Haney, himself a confirmed addict of the game, we've come up with this Guide to Michigan Public Golf Courses.

Golf has been popular in Michigan for a long time, long before the Bear and the Legend and the Monument and all of today's catchy names.

The Ann Arbor Golf & Outing Club says it has been playing golf since 1890. The University of Michigan's Alister Mackenzie-designed course, which wraps around AAG&O, is just a kid — it's 59 years old.

Scottish professional Alex Smith designed Wawashkamo on Mackinac Island's high ground for the summer cottagers in 1898 and it claims to be the oldest continuously-played nine holer in the state.

A turn-of-the century Grand Rapids and Indiana Railway brochure said "Those beautiful places in northern Michigan which are so attractive because of their natural locations and advantages are now of greater interest to lovers of the game of golf. This season the golf grounds are in better condition than ever and much care has been given them to put the courses in prime condition."

It was as easy then to lure golfers to Charlevoix, Petoskey, Harbor Springs and Mackinac Island as it is today.

Scots-born Donald Ross's first Michigan design opened for play in 1910. The course has gone through several name changes and today it's Rogell Golf Course, a Detroit municipal course where Chuck Kocsis, arguably the state's finest golfer, learned to play the game.

Ross, the game's premier designer, returned many times to Michigan during the nation's first golf boom, from 1916-31 when an average of 300 courses were built in the United States each year. Ross left us an array of superb courses including the state's best known championship course, Oakland Hills Country Club.

Most Ross courses are private but in addition to Rogell, he did Rackham, twice host to the United States Public Links Championship, for the city of Detroit and 36-hole Warren Valley for Wayne County. They haven't been as well cared for as the private clubs although better days seem to be ahead for both.

Los Angeles-based American Golf Corporation has leased Rackham, along with Chandler, Palmer and Rouge and the Rouge driving range, and said it would pump $2.5 million into maintenance and improvements in the next two years. Wayne County, with golf enthusiast Edward McNamara as County Executive, is taking steps to put Warren Valley in top shape.

Many of the state's daily fee courses were built in the second golf boom, from 1959-71. The National Golf Foundation said that the nation saw nearly 400 courses built during each year of the second boom. Among them was the Robert Trent Jones course which opened in 1965 at Boyne Highlands and triggered northern Michigan's resort golf industry.

Now we're in a third boom and it is resort and daily fee course driven in Michigan. The NGF lists 70 courses either under construction, ready to open or in the planning stage in Michigan and 55 of them are public. It's a bonanza for the state's golfers.

Some of the game's hottest designers are at work in the state —Tom Fazio and Arthur Hills, up-and-coming Tom Doak and regional designers Jerry Matthews, Bill Newcomb, Warner Bowen, Michael Hurdzan, Mark De Vries, Jeff Gornley and Harry Bowers.

We're a wetlands state with more than 11,000

lakes and more often than not, wetlands are involved in golf course design. The architects, working under strict Department of Natural Resources guidelines, are doing an imaginative job and the number of courses nominated annually for "Best New" in the golf magazines reflects it.

Pat Rielly, past president of the PGA of America, said after a Michigan visit a few years ago that "God makes the courses in Michigan." When you travel the state and see courses from Stonehedge near Kalamazoo to classic old Belvedere at Charlevoix, you'd be hard put to disagree.

The Guide is the most up-to-date compilation possible of public and resort golf in Michigan and it's more than a simple listing of location, yardage and telephone number. We want you to have a little feel for the courses you play and so we've given a brief description of them. You may be interested in finding what choices you have by categories such as scenic value, difficulty, best value or other special features — or where you get the best lessons, burgers or 19th hole atmosphere. So we have included a number of listings in the back of the book. On courses which either are not notable or neither I nor a trusted source has visited, only basic information is given.

HOW TO USE THIS GUIDE

The course listings in this Guide are organized by regions that consist of one or more counties. In the more heavily populated southeast Michigan area, Wayne and Oakland Counties are each treated as a separate region, Macomb and St. Clair Counties are combined as one region and Washtenaw, Livingston and Monroe Counties are combined as one region. In each region, individual courses are listed alphabetically within their corresponding county.

Included in the back of the Guide is a complete cross index of counties and regions, and an alphabetical list of public courses. Several courses advised us that their mailing address is in one county but the course itself is actually in another. Our book may list these courses under a different county than other guides.

In the listings, the following codes are used:

$—Greens fee to $15
$$—Greens fee to $25
$$$—Greens fee to $50 (usually includes cart)
$$$$—Greens fee more than $50 (includes cart)
Range—Driving range available
S—Slope rating at the middle course marker. (For a discussion of the slope rating system, please refer to "The Scoop on Slope" in the back of this Guide. Some 215 courses in Michigan had been rated entering 1991.)

Additional information about the amenities at each course is enclosed in brackets.

The author and the publisher have made every effort to ensure that the information in the Guide is accurate and up-to-date. This spring we were able to contact all but six of the courses to confirm addresses, phone numbers, par, yardage, greens fees, food and beverage service. Nevertheless, the information is subject to change. It is always wise to call ahead and at many courses you must do so to confirm tee times.

We value your suggestions on how to make future editions of this Guide as useful as possible. We will be especially appreciative to learn of any errors that you may find.

WAYNE COUNTY

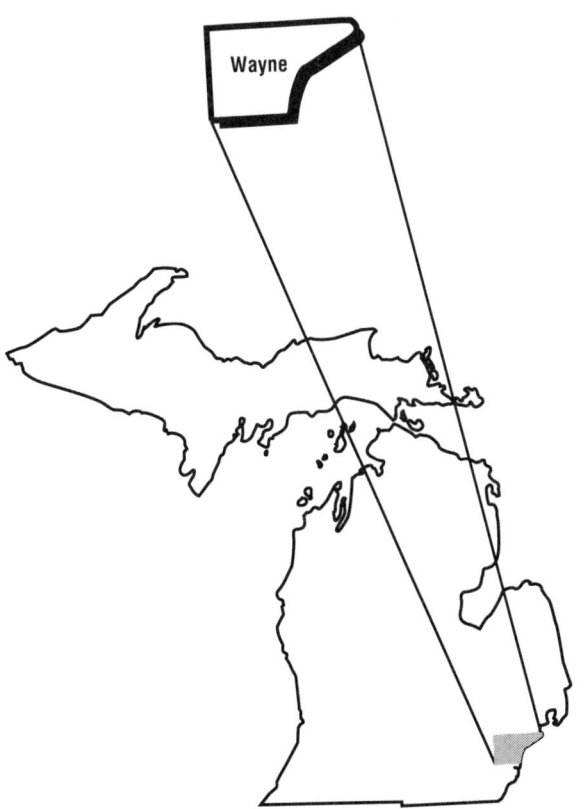

WAYNE COUNTY

BELLE ISLE GOLF COURSE (9)
Belle Isle Park, Detroit. (313) 267-7130.
Great location for a course but hasn't had any tender loving care in years. Flat and uninspiring.
Par 29, 1881 yards. Range $

BONNIE BROOK GOLF COURSE (18)
Telegraph Rd., bet. 7 & 8 Mile Rds., Detroit. (313) 538-8383.
Busy par 64 short course (4190 yards) except when Rouge River is up — then it's underwater because it's flood plain. Ego-builder if they'd cut the greens.
$ *[bar, grill, banquet facilities]*

BROOKLANE GOLF COURSE (18)
6 Mile & Sheldon, Northville. (313) 348-1010.
Holster the artillery — it's par 61 and 4,008 yards.
Range $ *[bar, grill]*

CHANDLER PARK GOLF COURSE (18)
Chandler Park Dr. & Dickerson, Detroit. (313) 267-7150.
Detroit muny is bordered by Ford Freeway that helped reduce it to 4615 yards and par 68. A favorite of East Side retirees and seniors.
$ *[bar, grill]*

DEARBORN HILLS GOLF COURSE (18)
Telegraph Rd., north of Michigan, Dearborn. (313) 277-9625.
Donated to city by Mrs. Robert Herndon and Warner Bowen was hired to remodel course that is shoehorned into 97 acres. Bowen plans a challenging par 60 executive course. Work begins this spring.
Par 69, 5600 yards. $ *[grill]*

DUN ROVIN (9)
16377 Haggerty Rd., Plymouth. (313) 420-0144.
Was an 18-holer and developer eliminated nine for condos. Now it's 3100 yards max and par 35. $

FELLOWS CREEK GOLF COURSE (27)
2936 Lotz Rd., Canton. (313) 728-1300.
Three fairly equal nines of 3200 yards from the back, 3000 from the middle. No. 1 handicap hole on two of the nines is a 200-yard, par 3.
Par 36. Slope: E/W nines 119; S/W 116, S/E 118.
$$ *[bar, grill]*

FOX CREEK GOLF COURSE (18)
36000 W. 7 Mile Rd., Livonia. (313) 471-3400.
City of Livonia's third course and no city in the state has done a better job of operating its courses. Mark De Vries designed Fox Creek as he did Whispering Willows and it has a little more character.
Par 71, 6612 yards. S119. $$ *[restaurant]*

GLENHURST GOLF COURSE (18)
6 Mile Rd., west of Telegraph, Redford Township. (313) 592-8758.
With five par 3s, longest 177 and down to 116, it's home of the Hole-in-One. No course in metropolitan Detroit yields more aces. Glenhurst is popular and has been well maintained.
Par 70, 5600 yards. S107. $$ *[bar, grill]*

HARBOUR CLUB GOLF COURSE (9)
48356 Denton, Belleville. (313) 699-8844.
Along I-94 in the apartment/condo land west of Metropolitan Airport.
Par 36, 3286 yards. Range $$

HAWTHORNE VALLEY GOLF COURSE (9)
7300 N. Merriman, Westland. (313) 422-3440.
Got scrunched years ago by the Ann Arbor Trail and checks in under 2,900 yards.
Par 3. $

HILLTOP GOLF COURSE (18)
Beck Rd., south of M-14, Plymouth. (313) 453-9800.
The fastest greens you'll find on a public course. Operator-pro John Jawor likes 'em that way but the fourth green, slanted into the top of a hill, is IMPOSSIBLE with pin in front. Miss it and ball trickles down, down, down as temper goes up, up, up. Aaarrrgh! Well-maintained.
Par 70, 6400 yards. S119. $$ *[bar, grill]*

IDYL WYLD (18)
5 Mile Rd., bet. Newburgh & Farmington Rds., Livonia. (313) 464-6325.
City's first muny — they bought an existing course. It's tight and you've got to stay alert.
Par 70, 5817 yards. S115. $ *[bar, grill]*

LOWER HURON PAR 3 (18)
In Lower Huron Metro Park, Belleville. (313) 697-9181.
Fine for beginners.
Par 54, 1372 yards. $

MISSION HILLS GOLF CLUB (18)
Sheldon Rd., north of M-14, Plymouth. (313) 453-1047.
On grounds of former St. John Seminary. Nine holes built by late Cardinal Mooney and designed by Oakland Hills patriarch Al Watrous for the clergy. Nine holes added later.
Par 71, 6500 yards. S113. $$ *[bar, grill]*

OASIS GOLF CENTER (18)
5 Mile Rd., bet. I-275 & Haggerty Rd., Plymouth. (313) 420-4653.
Wayne County Executive Ed McNamara, a golf nut and man behind Livonia's strong municipal program when he was mayor, is part owner of the 2200-yard, par 3. Range is domed in winter and you'd better hurry. Headed for development.
Range $

PALMER PARK GOLF COURSE (18)
Woodward at 7 Mile Rd., Detroit. (313) 883-2525.
Flat track. Typical of Detroit munys — needs TLC.
Par 69, 5729 yards. $ *[snacks]*

PINE CREEK COUNTRY CLUB (18)
50521 W. Huron River Dr., Belleville. (313) 483-5010.
Well-kept.
Par 3, 2765 yards. $ *[bar, grill]*

RIVERVIEW HIGHLANDS GOLF COURSE (27)
15015 Sibley Rd., Riverview. (313) 479-2266.
First 18 designed by Bill Newcomb and built around "Mt. Trashmore," Riverview's ski hill atop a land fill. Other nine designed by Art Hills and that's a pretty heady combination for muny operation but Riverview's recreation department has been one of the state's leaders.
Par 36, 3000 yards. Gold/Blue S111, Gold/Red S111, Red/Blue S115. $ *[bar, grill]*

ROGELL GC (18)
Berg Rd., bet. Grand River & 7 Mile, Detroit. (313) 935-5332.
Course manager Carl Towne has struggled against lack of city money and done quite a good job — this is only city 18-holer not part of new lease package with American Golf Corp. which begins this season. Originally known as Phoenix Country Club and then Redford Municipal, course was designed by Donald Ross and you still can get some Ross glimpses. Par 3, 142-yard 15th hole next to the clubhouse is home of annual Detroit News Hole-in-One Contest. Rouge River fronts the green and devours timid shots.
Par 70, 6018 yards. *$ [bar, grill]*

ROUGE PARK GOLF COURSE (18)
Burt & Plymouth Rds., Detroit. (313) 935-5285.
Another muny where the manager struggled to give the public decent conditions but it was an uphill fight and American Golf Corp. takes over this year. Has some very good holes and a tricky 97-yard, par 3 that surrenders a lot of aces. The shooter rarely sees the ball go in because the green is so much higher than the tee.
Par 72, 6327 yards. Range *$ [snacks]*

SHADY HOLLOW GOLF COURSE (18)
Wayne Rd., bet. Ecorse Rd. & Wick, north of I-94, Romulus. (313) 721-0430.
Fast track.
Par 72, 6100 yards. *$ [bar, grill]*

SOUTHGATE MUNICIPAL GOLF COURSE (18)
14600 Reaume Parkway, north of Eureka Rd., Southgate. (313) 246-1358.
Muny operation, good beginners, couples, seniors course.
Par 58, 3427 yards. Range *$*

SULTANA PAR 3 (18)
22201 Pennsylvania, Wyandotte. (313) 285-7480.
Par 3, 2518 yards. *$ [bar, grill]*

TALL OAKS GOLF COURSE (18)
14310 Wahrman Rd., Romulus. (313) 941-3372.
You can spot it from I-275 and from the air taking off from Metropolitan Airport. Tall oaks but short holes.
Par 56, 2633 yards. *$ [snacks]*

TAYLOR MEADOWS GOLF CLUB (18)
25360 Ecorse Rd., Taylor. (313) 295-0507.
Art Hills designed it on a piece of undesirable property and has given Taylor a jewel that will only get better with time. It borders I-94 freeway just west of Telegraph.
Par 71, 6057 yards. S110. *$$ [bar, grill]*

WARREN VALLEY GOLF COURSE (36)
Warren, west of Beech Rd., Dearborn Heights. (313) 561-1040. A pair of old Donald Ross courses that still show some Ross touches. Owned by Wayne County which slooooowly but surely is getting the heavily-played courses into shape.
Par 72, 5880 yards; par 71, 5827. *$$ [bar, grill]*

WESTLAND MUNICIPAL GOLF COURSE (9)
Merriman, south of Cherry Hill, Westland. (313) 721-6660.
Typical muny: leagues, seniors, comfortable par 34, 2688 yards.
$ [sandwiches, beer]

WHISPERING WILLOWS GOLF CLUB (18)
Newburgh Rd. at 8 Mile, Livonia. (313) 476-4493.
Well-operated, full-sized muny with range and country club flavor thanks to a city that sees golf as an asset.
Par 71, 6520 yards. S108. Range *$ [bar, grill]*

WILLOW METROPARK GOLF COURSE (18)
22900 Huron River Dr., east of I-275, New Boston. (313) 753-4040 or (800) 23-GOLF4.
Ann Arbor architect Bill Newcomb did a good job — best design of all the Huron Clinton Metropark courses. And if you like jetliners, well, depending on the wind, they can be overhead constantly going into Metro.
Par 71, 6378 yards. S122. *$ [snacks]*

WOODSIDE MEADOWS GOLF COURSE (18)
20820 Inkster Rd., Romulus. (313) 782-5136.
Real short.
Par 61, 3853 yards. *$ [bar, grill]*

OAKLAND COUNTY

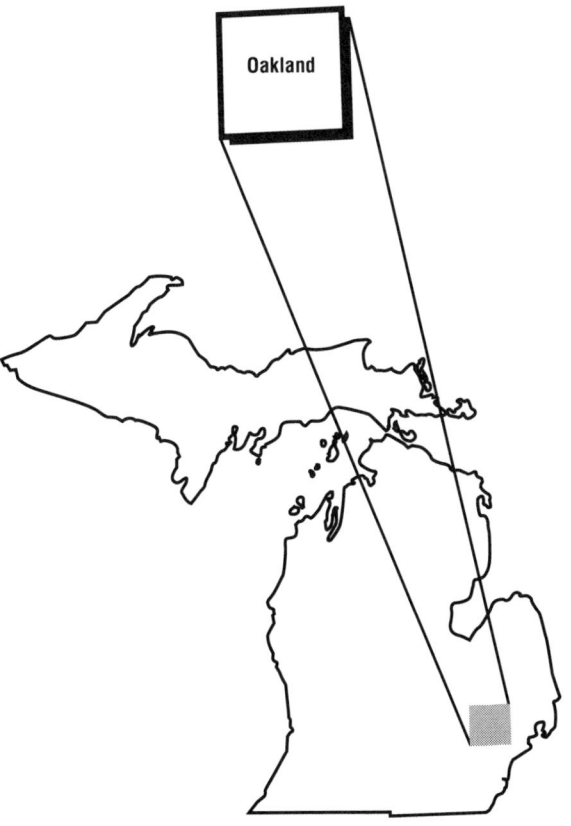

OAKLAND COUNTY

ARROWHEAD GOLF CLUB (27)
2797 Lapeer Rd., at I-75, Auburn Hills. (313) 373-6860.
It's green, it's busy, it's unremarkable. Three par 36, 3200-yard nines.
$$ [bar, grill]

BALD MOUNTAIN GOLF COURSE (18)
3350 Kern Rd., Lake Orion. (313) 373-1110.
Par 71, 6800-yard course operated by Prieskorn family, active locally for more than half a century because they know their business. Also have a 9-hole executive course. Designed by Wilfrid Reid and William Connellan who once was construction boss for Donald Ross. They also did Indianwood and Plum Hollow. Nuf said.
S115. Range *$$ [bar, grill]*

BEECH WOODS GOLF CENTER (9)
Beech Rd., bet. 8 & 9 Mile Rds., Southfield. (313) 354-4786.
My neighborhood course and I can't say anything good about it. Poorly designed par 35, 2900 yards.
Range *$ [bar, grill]*

BOGIE LAKE GOLF CLUB (18)
11231 Bogie Lake Rd., Union Lake. (313) 363-4449.
Short and hilly but no pushover.
Par 71, 6145 yards. S120. *$ [bar, grill]*

BRAMBLEWOOD GOLF COURSE (18)
2154 Bramblewood Rd., Holly. (313) 634-3481.
Par 70, 6000 yards. *$ [bar, grill]*

CLARKSTON GOLF CLUB (9)
9241 N. Eston, Clarkston. (313) 394-0020.
Well-kept 2700-yard, par 35 that ends with a 140-yard, par 3.
S100. *$ [bar, grill]*

DUNHAM HILLS GOLF CLUB (18)
13561 Dunham Rd., Milford. (313) 887-9170.
Par 72, 6800-yarder one of best and toughest in metro area. Hilly. Hosted many Michigan Publinx championships.
S120. *$$$ [bar, grill]*

EL DORADO GOLF COURSE (18)
2869 N. Pontiac Trail, Walled Lake. (313) 624-1736.
Second nine opens this year with some water to go with two ponds that are in play on three holes on the front. Length around 6000 yards.
Par 35, 3055 yards. Range $ [bar]

EVERGREEN HILLS (9)
Evergreen at Southfield Civic Center, Southfield. (313) 354-4787.
Southfield muny. Very busy. Unremarkable.
Par 34, 2900 yards. $

GLENLORE GOLF COURSE (18)
2000 Sleeth Rd., Milford. (313) 363-7997.
Par 3, 2200 yards. $ [snacks]

GLEN OAKS GOLF COURSE (18)
30500 W. 13 Mile Rd., Farmington Hills. (313) 851-8356.
Busiest of Oakland County Rec Department's four courses but not the best. Major drainage project begins this year and should improve the par 70, 5837-yarder.
$$ [bar, grill]

HAMPTON GOLF CLUB (9)
2600 Club Dr., Rochester Hills. (313) 852-3250.
Condo course.
Par 32, 2000 yards. $

HARLEY'S GOLF COURSE & RESTAURANT (27)
2280 Union Lake Rd., Union Lake. (313) 363-0201.
Three nines of 2665 (par 35), 2632 (par 36) and 3215 (par 37) yards.
$

HARTLAND GLEN GOLF & COUNTRY CLUB (27)
12400 Highland Rd. (M-59), Hartland. (313) 887-3777.
Nines of 2770 (par 35), 3120 (par 35) and 3160 (par 36) yards. Maturing, getting better.
S113. Range $$

HEATHER HIGHLANDS GOLF CLUB (18)
11450 E. Holly Rd., at I-75, Holly. (313) 634-6800.
Pleasant course, rolling, designed by Chicagoan Robert Bruce Harris in 1962 and originally known as Holly Greens. Also have a nine-hole short course (par 31, 2052 yards). Carts mandatory.
Par 72, 6845 yards. S117. Range $$ [bar, grill]

HICKORY HILL GOLF CLUB (9)
2307 Orland, Wixom. (313) 624-4733.
Excellent condition by Michigan Publinxer George Catto. Two very tough par 3s. Good value.
Par 35, 3000 yards. $ [grill]

HIGHLAND HILLS GOLF CLUB (18)
2075 Oakland Dr., Highland. (313) 887-4481.
Par 72, 6186 yards. $$ [bar, grill]

INDEPENDENCE GREEN EXECUTIVE GOLF COURSE (18)
Grand River at Halsted, Farmington Hills. (313) 471-6800.
Apartment course by Bruce Matthews.
Par 56, 3500 yards. $

INDIAN SPRINGS GOLF COURSE (18)
5100 Indian Trail, Clarkston. (313) 625-7870.
One of newest Huron Clinton Metropolitan Authority courses and typical Metropark course. Nice topography, not a lot of difficulty except for crowned greens which shows in-house designer's lack of understanding of golf. Nice clubhouse and Elias Brothers food service as at all Metroparks.
Par 71, 6707 yards. Range $ [snacks]

KENSINGTON METROPARKS GOLF COURSE (18)
I-96 & Kensington Rd., Milford. (313) 685-9332.
Prototype Metropark course. Nice, rolling, busy, not too difficult.
Par 71, 6381 yards. S115. $ [grill]

LINCOLN HILLS GOLF COURSE (9)
2666 W. 14 Mile Rd., Birmingham. (313) 647-4468.
Locals call it adjacent Birmingham Country Club's West Course. Nice nine-holer by Bruce Matthews. Birmingham residents only.
Par 35, 3001 yards. S122. $

LINKS OF NOVI (27)
10 Mile Rd., bet. Beck & Napier Rds., Novi. (313) 380-9595.
A 27-hole course developed by Livonia pro Gary Whitener and partners, and designed by Jerry Matthews. Looks flat from the road but some stunning elevation changes in woods. Nine holes scheduled for May opening, second nine perhaps mid-summer and hope to have third nine open in fall.
Par 72, 6500 yards first 18; par 34, 3000 yards third nine. S120. Range *$$*

LINKS AT PINEWOOD GOLF CLUB (18)
8600 PGA Drive, Walled Lake. (313) 669-9800.
Primarily an outing course designed by owner Ernie Fuller and it's busy. Nice clubhouse and lockers.
Par 70, 6225 yards. *$$$ [bar, grill]*

MULBERRY HILLS COUNTRY CLUB (18)
3530 Noble Rd., Oxford. (313) 628-2808.
Open, some water.
Par 73, 6400 yards. $

OXFORD HILLS GOLF & COUNTRY CLUB (18)
300 E. Drahner, Oxford. (313) 628-2518.
Couple of stiff par 5s of 530 and 567 (whites) and par 3s (198 and 186).
Par 72, 6522 yards. S117. *$$*

PEBBLE CREEK GOLF CLUB (18)
24095 Currie Rd., at 10 Mile, South Lyon. (313) 437-5411.
Second nine opens this year in developing 10 Mile Rd. corridor. Designed by Bill Newcomb.
Par 72, 6200 yards. *$$ [bar, grill]*

PINE KNOB GOLF COURSE (18)
5580 Waldon Rd., Clarkston. (313) 625-4430.
King Kong first tee. Course has matured well, good mixture of holes, big tees, big greens. One of best in metro area.
Par 71, 6618 yards. *$$$*

PINE TRACE GOLF CLUB (18)
South Blvd., east of Adams, Rochester Hills. (313) 852-7100.
Art Hills design with a lot of northern Michigan flavor. Could be best public course in metro area — serious golfers operate it. Well-maintained and you'd better play FAST. Play first nine in 2:15 or be told to leave. Downside is that carts are required and cart path restrictions mean you've got to hit 'n' run and carry a handful of clubs. Carts required.
Par 72, 6610 yards. S127. Range *$$$ [bar, grill]*

PONTIAC COUNTRY CLUB (18)
4335 Elizabeth Lake Rd., Pontiac. (313) 682-6333.
Hands-on operation by Syron family makes for homey touch. Well-maintained and home of popular 54-hole Syron Memorial Tournament on Fourth of July weekend. Area's best amateurs never rip it up.
Par 72, 6324 yards. S118. Range *$$ [bar, grill]*

PONTIAC MUNICIPAL GOLF COURSE (18)
800 Golf Dr., Pontiac. (313) 858-8990.
No. 1 handicap hole is 217-yard, par 3 second. Have five other par 3s and only one is short, 123 yard 13th.
Par 69, 5689 yards. *$ [bar, grill]*

RACKHAM GOLF COURSE (18)
10100 W. 10 Mile Rd., Huntington Woods. (313) 543-4040.
Next to the Detroit Zoo along I-696 freeway. Designed by Donald Ross and fallen on hard times under City of Detroit operation. Sad. Still some fine Ross holes — 10th, 11th and 16th through 18th.
Par 71, 6130 yards. S113. *$ [snacks]*

RED OAKS GOLF COURSE (9)
29600 John R, Madison Heights. (313) 541-5030.
Good use of land along Red Run drain. owned by Oakland County Rec Department. Also state's first dome range.
Par 31, 2100 yards. Range *$*

ROCHESTER HILLS GOLF & COUNTRY CLUB (18)
655 Michelson, Rochester Hills. (313) 852-4800.
Thirteen water crossings on popular par 72, 6500-yard course, one of the region's old-timers.
S121. *$$ [bar, grill]*

SAN MARINO GOLF COURSE (9)
26634 Halsted Rd., Farmington Hills. (313) 476-5910.
Increasingly busy as subdivisions pop up. Another Matthews course.
Par 36, 3300 yards. $ *[bar, grill]*

SHENANDOAH COUNTRY CLUB (18)
5600 Walnut Lake Rd., West Bloomfield. (313) 682-4300.
One of early Jerry Matthews designs. Front side has some tight side-by-side holes, back some nice treed holes. New owners putting substantial money into sorely-needed improvements and greens fees jump. Carts required.
Par 72, 7000 yards. S128. $$$ *[bar, grill]*

SILVER LAKE GOLF CLUB (9)
2602 W. Walton Blvd., Pontiac. (313) 673-1611.
Short but some nice holes.
Par 36, 3100 yards. S117. $ *[bar, grill]*

SPRINGDALE GOLF COURSE (9)
300 Strathmore, Birmingham. (313) 646-0480.
Owned by city of Birmingham. For residents only.
Par 33, 2798 yards. S113. $

SPRINGFIELD OAKS GOLF COURSE (18)
12450 Andersonville Rd., Davisburg. (313) 625-2540.
Best of Oakland County Rec Dept. courses, hilly, longer, tougher than county's other courses. Added some new bunkers and put sprinklers in rough to toughen it.
Par 72, 6320 yards. $ *[bar, grill]*

SPRING LAKE GOLF COURSE (18)
6060 Maybee Rd., Clarkston. (313) 625-3731.
Basically wide open, popular league course.
Par 72, 6520 yards. S117. $$ *[bar, grill]*

STONEY CREEK METROPARK (18)
4300 Main Park Rd., 2 miles west of M-53, Washington. (313) 781-4242.
Very busy.
Par 72, 6648 yards. S121. $ *[grill]*

SYLVAN GLEN GOLF COURSE (18)
5725 Rochester Rd., Troy. (313) 879-0040.
Troy's well-kept municipal course. Water crossings on a dozen holes. Good restaurant.
Par 70, 6554 yards. S115. *$ [restaurant]*

TANGLEWOOD GOLF CLUB (18)
53503 10 Mile Rd., at Chubb Rd., South Lyon. (313) 486-3355.
Opens this year at 6800 yards and par 72. *$$$*

WESTBROOKE GOLF COURSE (18)
47666 Grand River, Novi. (313) 349-2723.
Formerly Bob O Link.
Par 70, 6100 yards. *$ [bar, grill]*

WHITE LAKE OAKS GOLF COURSE (18)
991 Williams Lake Rd., just south of M-59, Union Lake. (313) 698-2700.
Nicely treed with plenty of specimen oaks. Comfortable course, comfortable atmosphere. Oakland County Rec Department's second busiest course is much superior to busier Glen Oaks.
Par 70, 5767 yards. *$ [bar, grill]*

$ — Greens fee to $15
$$ — Greens fee to $25
$$$ — Greens fee to $50
$$$$ — Greens fee more than $50
Range — Driving range available
S — Slope rating

MACOMB & ST. CLAIR COUNTIES

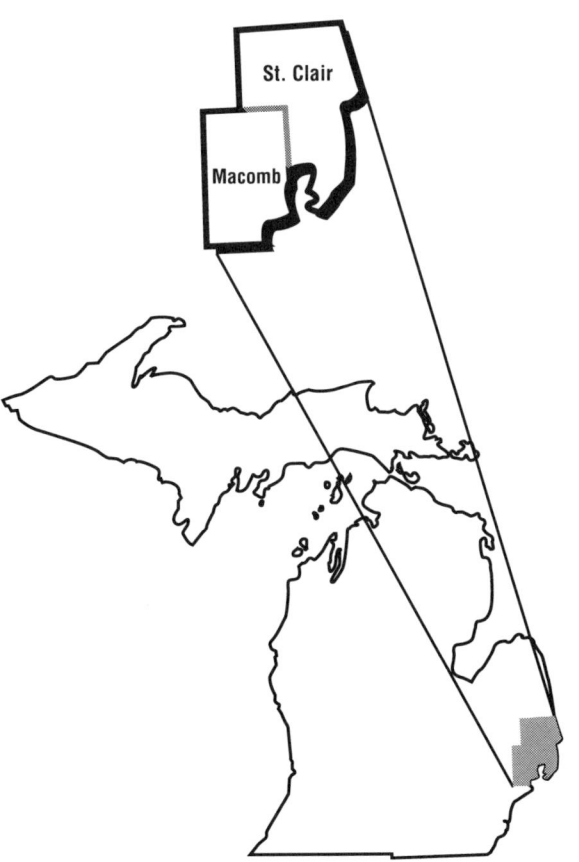

MACOMB COUNTY

BELLO WOODS GOLF COURSE (27)
23650 23 Mile Rd., Mt. Clemens. (313) 949-1200.
Branch of the Clinton River affects play on seven holes of the Red and White nines while the Gold nine is tree-lined and northern Michigan flavored.
Par 36, 3100 yards. *$ [bar, grill]*

BRUCE HILLS GOLF CLUB (18)
6771 Taft Rd., Romeo. (313) 752-7244.
Another short one. Near Ford proving ground northwest of Romeo.
Par 70, 5800 yards. S107. *$ [bar, rooms available]*

CEDAR GLEN GOLF CLUB (18)
36860 25 Mile Rd., New Baltimore. (313) 725-8156.
Flat stuff on north end of town.
Par 71, 6607 yards. *$ [bar, grill]*

CRACKLEWOOD GOLF CLUB (18)
18215 24 Mile Rd., Mt. Clemens. (313) 781-0808.
Jerry Matthews design which elevates it above the ordinary. Owners came up with the name during construction process when they cracked some practice shots off the trees which should tell you something about tightness.
Par 72, 6684 yards. Range *$ [bar, grill]*

FERN HILL GOLF & COUNTRY CLUB (18)
17600 Clinton River Rd., Mt. Clemens. (313) 286-4700.
Clinton River flood plain and a lot of holes-in-one.
Par 70, 6000 yards. S113. *$ [bar, grill]*

HEATHER HILLS GOLF COURSE (9)
3100 McKail Rd., Almont. (313) 798-3120.
Second nine scheduled this season.
Par 35, 3400 yards. Range *$ [bar, grill]*

HICKORY HOLLOW GOLF COURSE (18)
4901 North Ave., at 22 Mile Rd., Mt. Clemens. (313) 949-9033.
Clinton River often in play on par 73 (five par 5s), 6200-yard course.
S107. *$$ [bar, grill]*

MAPLE LANE GOLF COURSE (54)
14 Mile & Hoover, Sterling Heights. (313) 795-4000.
Home of year-round golf and many, many maples. Busiest complex in metro Detroit especially at league time — wagon train time. Won't host the Open but well-maintained.
Courses are 5781 yards (par 70), 5926 yards (par 71) and 6154 yards (par 71). North S108, West S111. *$$ [bar, grill]*

METRO BEACH GOLF COURSE (18)
31300 Metro Parkway, Mt. Clemens. (313) 463-4581.
Generic Metropark par 3 of 1153 yards. *$*

NORTHBROOK GOLF CLUB (18)
21690 27 Mile Rd., Washington. (313) 749-3415.
Good stretch of holes in the middle and the ever-present Clinton River, Macomb County's favorite waterway.
Par 72, 6400 yards. S116. *$$ [bar, grill]*

OAK RIDGE GOLF CLUB (18)
26 Mile Rd. at I-94, New Haven. (313) 749-5151.
Flat and open par 72, 6800 yards. No. 1 handicap hole is 18th, 444-yard, par 4 from middle marker. Range *$ [restaurant]*

PARTRIDGE CREEK GOLF CLUB (54)
43843 Romeo Plank Rd., south of M-59 (Hall Rd.), Mt. Clemens. (313) 286-9822.
Load 'em up, move 'em out.
Three par 72 courses of 6015, 6025 and 6405 yards. Blue S114, Green S103, Red S112. *$ [bar, grill]*

PINE BROOK GOLF COURSE (9)
County Line Rd. & 29 Mile, Richmond. (313) 727-7029.
Ego builder with junior and senior rates.
Par 36, 3000 yards. *$ [bar, grill]*

PINE VALLEY GOLF CLUB (27)
31 Mile Rd. & Romeo Plank Rd., Romeo. (313) 752-9633.
Doc McKinley the dentist did it — his son carries on the tradition on the west side of the state with Brigadoon.
Red/Blue: par 36, 3106 yards; Blue/Gold: par 36, 2911 yards; Blue/Gold: par 35, 2950 yards. Red/Blue S116, Red/Gold S110, Blue/Gold S107. Range *$$*
[bar, grill]

PLUM BROOK GOLF CLUB (18)
13390 Plumbrook Dr., Sterling Heights. (313) 264-9411.
Beaupre family has been in business for years and takes pride in its 6226-yard, par 71 course.
S108. *$$ [bar, grill]*

RAMMLER COUNTRY CLUB (18)
38180 Utica Rd., Sterling Heights. (313) 264-4101.
Popular East Side fast track.
Par 71 and 6298 yards from the back. S108. Range *$$ [bar, grill]*

ROMEO GOLF COURSE (18)
14600 E. 32 Mile Rd., Romeo. (313) 752-9673.
Owner Joe Karam making improvements, rebuilding tees, adding a second course which will be ready in 1993.
Par 72, 6000 yards. Range *$$ [bar, grill, restaurant]*

SALT RIVER GOLF COURSE (18)
33633 23 Mile Rd., New Baltimore. (313) 725-0311.
Flat but river in play on most of front nine plus 10 and 18.
Par 71, 6107 yards. S112. *$$*

SPRING BROOK GOLF CLUB (9)
42545 Ryan Rd., Sterling Heights. (313) 739-6230.
Tom Watson is the pro. Honest.
Par 36, 3100 yards. *$ [bar]*

SUNNYBROOK GOLF, BOWLING & MOTEL (27)
7191 17 Mile Rd., Sterling Heights. (313) 977-9759.
Nines of 2800 (par 34), 2900 (par 36) and 3400 (par 36) yards. They go from bowling alleys in winter to course in summer and back. Unremarkable. *$$*

TEE J'S GOLF COURSE (9)
21111 23 Mile Rd., Mt. Clemens. (313) 598-5010.
Short stuff, one nine par 36, 2929 yards and another nine 1373-yard, par 3.
$ [bar, grill]

WARFIELD GREENS GOLF CLUB (9)
34255 Utica Rd., Fraser. (313) 293-9887.
Par 29, 1600 yards. *$*

ST. CLAIR COUNTY

BELLE RIVER GOLF & COUNTRY CLUB (18)
12564 Belle River Rd., Memphis. (313) 392-2121.
Eight holes bordered by the Belle River and a lake is in play on five holes of the par 72, 6750 yard course.
Range *$ [bar, grill]*

FORT GRATIOT GOLF RESORT (9)
5741 Lake Shore Rd., Port Huron. (313) 385-3542.
Par 36, 3000 yards.

LEANING TREE GOLF CLUB (18)
7890 Smiths Creek Rd., Smiths Creek. (313) 367-3528.
Par 72, 5757 yards. *$ [bar, grill]*

MARYSVILLE GOLF COURSE (18)
2080 River Rd., at Cuttle Rd., Marysville. (313) 364-4653.
Check out the ore carriers on the river and your score on this well-kept muny. Good variety of par 3s. 6500-yard, par 72. S116. *$ [hot dogs]*

MIDDLE CHANNEL COUNTRY CLUB (18)
2306 Golf Course Rd., Harsens Island. (313) 748-9922.
Island golf with some river breezes. One mile right from the ferry.
Par 72, 6100 yards. *$$ [bar, grill]*

MILL CREEK GOLF COURSE (9)
15886 Speaker Rd., Imlay City. (313) 395-7495.
Par 36, 3030 yards. *$ [grill, snacks]*

PINE SHORES GOLF CLUB (9)
709 Fred Moore Hwy., St. Clair. (313) 329-4294.
Nice little course a hop, skip and jump from the big freighters.
Par 35, 2800 yards. *$ [snacks]*

RATTLE RUN GOLF COURSE (18)
7163 St. Clair Hwy., St. Clair. (313) 329-2070.
Owner-pro Lou Powers' challenging design put it on *Golf Digest's* list of 75 best public courses in U.S. Maintenance sometimes doesn't keep pace with design.
Par 72, 6981 yards. S135. Range *$$ [bar, grill]*

WILLOW RIDGE GOLF CLUB (9)
3311 N. River Rd., Port Huron. (313) 982-7010.
Par 35, 2900 yards. *$ [bar, grill]*

WASHTENAW, LIVINGSTON & MONROE COUNTIES

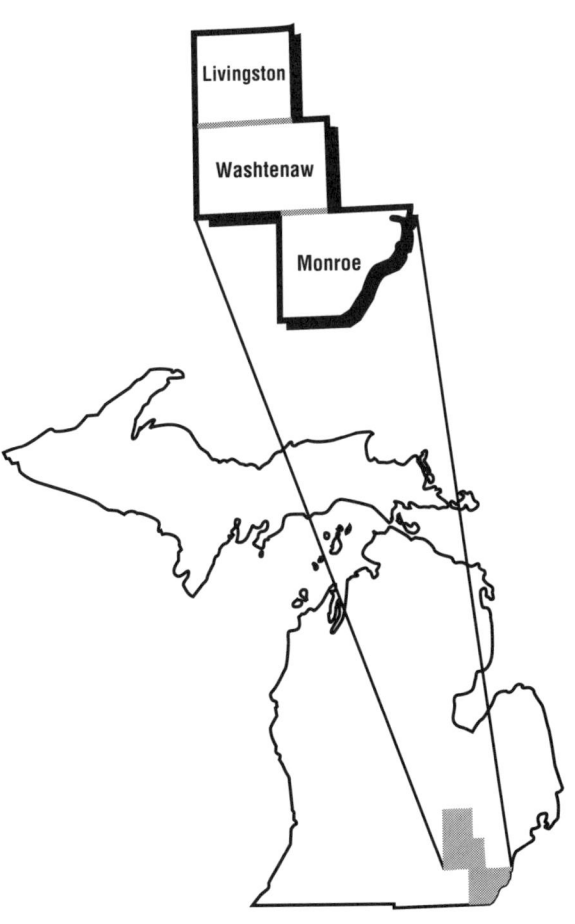

WASHTENAW COUNTY

BRAE BURN GOLF COURSE (18)
10860 W. 5 Mile Rd., at Napier, Plymouth. (313) 453-1900.
An old (1920s) collaboration of Wilfrid Reid and William Connellan, like Indianwood, Bald Mountain and Plum Hollow. No. 1 handicap hole is "The Monster," a 610-yard (whites) double dogleg par 5 with water on the left of first leg.
Par 70, 6311 yards. S118. *$$ [bar, grill]*

BROOKSIDE GOLF COURSE (18)
6437 Ann Arbor-Saline Rd., Saline. (313) 429-4276.
Lots of short par 4s — 315, 285, 325 (twice), 290 and 292 from the whites but there is that brook to contend with.
Par 71, 6112 yards. Range *$ [bar, grill]*

FOX HILLS COUNTRY CLUB (45)
8768 N. Territorial Rd., Plymouth. (313) 453-7272.
The Dul family had 27 nice holes and then they hired Art Hills to give them 18 terrific ones they call Golden Fox. It's pricier, in that $35-$45 range with cart, and it tells you right off that it's something special. Duffers will lose some balls but so did Hills when he played it during its 1989 opening. Golden Fox is par 72 with multiple tees up to 6783 yards and S129. Other nines are 3064, 3334 and 3450 yards. Range *$$ & $$$ [bar, grill]*

GREEN OAKS (18)
1775 E. Clark Rd., west of Ridge Rd., Ypsilanti. (313) 485-0881.
Par 71, 6800 yards. S120. *$ [grill, snacks]*

HICKORY WOODS (9)
5415 Crane Rd., Ypsilanti. (313) 434-GOLF.
Short stuff.
Par 35, 2715 yards. *$ [snacks]*

HUDSON MILLS GOLF COURSE (18)
4800 Dexter-Pinckney Rd., Dexter. (313) 426-8211.
Huron Clinton Metropark course. Pleasant, no big trouble.
Par 71, 6600 yards. *$ [grill]*

HURON GOLF CLUB (18)
1275 Huron St., at Radisson Resort, Exit 183 off I-94, Ypsilanti. (313) 487-2441.
Eastern Michigan University course designed by Karl Litten. Ford Lake usually is in view but out of play. However, there are ponds and wetlands and three in a row of the strangest holes around, the ninth (where does it go?), the 10th (where does it go?) and the 11th (where does it go?).
Par 72, 6750 yards. Range *$$ [bar, grill]*

HURON HILLS GOLF COURSE (18)
3465 E. Huron River Dr., Ann Arbor. (313) 971-6840.
Ann Arbor municipal. Back nine very hilly, front gently rolling. Strong senior and women's play.
Par 68, 5200 yards. *$ [snacks]*

LESLIE PARK GOLF COURSE (18)
2120 Traver Rd., north side of Ann Arbor. (313) 994-1163.
Very nice, well-kept muny featuring Cardiac Hill, the 442-yard straight up (it seems) 14th. Good test, good value.
Par 72, 6400 yards. S122. *$ [grill]*

PINEVIEW GOLF COURSE (27)
5820 Stony Creek Rd., 1-1/2 miles south of I-94 Exit 183, Ypsilanti. (313) 481-0500.
Opened in 1990 and back nine has northern flavor, rolling and pines. Also has executive nine-hole course of 1853 yards.
Par 72, 6283 yards. Range *$$ [bar, grill]*

REDDEMAN FARMS GOLF COURSE (18)
555 S. Dancer Rd. at Jerusalem Rd., Chelsea. (313) 475-3020.
Opened late in the 1990 season on 200-year-old farm just south of I-94. No. 1 handicap hole is par 4 ninth with last 100 yards over water.
Par 72, 6487 yards. *$$*

ROLLING HILLS GOLF COURSE (9)
3990 Willis Rd., Milan. (313) 434-0600.
Short and fast.
Par 33, 2470 yards. *$ [bar, grill]*

ROLLING MEADOWS COUNTRY CLUB (18)
6484 Sutton Rd., Whitmore Lake. (313) 662-5144.
Rustic renovated original farm clubhouse. Pleasant.
Par 70, 6400 yards. $ *[snacks]*

RUSTIC GLEN GOLF COURSE (9)
12090 W. Michigan Ave., Saline. (313) 429-7679.
Short stuff, nice range. Par 36, 3100 yards.
Range $ *[bar, grill]*

SALEM HILLS GOLF CLUB (18)
8810 W. 6 Mile Rd., at Currie, Northville. (313) 437-2152.
A good, solid, no-nonsense, no-gimmicks golf course that long has ranked as one of the state's best public courses. Has hosted Buick Open and U.S. Publinx qualifiers. An early (1961) collaboration of the Bruce-Jerry Matthews father-son team.
Par 72, 6900 yards. S116. Range $$ *[bar, grill]*

LIVINGSTON COUNTY

DAMA GOLF CLUB (18)
410 Marr Rd., north of Howell. (517) 546-4635.
Par 72, 6500 yards. Range $$ *[bar, grill]*

FAULKWOOD GOLF CLUB (18)
300 S. Hughes Rd., north of Grand River, Howell. (517) 546-4180.
Country Club flavor, well-maintained and challenging par 72, 7045-yarder (whites). Good three-hole finish of 210-yard, par 3; 540-yard, par 5; and 460-yard, par 4, 18th usually into the wind with a pond short of the green that cuts all the way to the center of the fairway.
Range $$ *[bar, grill]*

HURON MEADOWS GOLF COURSE (18)
8765 Hammel Rd., south of Brighton. (313) 231-4084.
Typical Huron-Clinton Metropark course. Broad fairways, generally good maintenance and few hazards.
Par 72, 6600 yards. Range $ *[grill]*

IRONWOOD GOLF CLUB (9)
6902 Highland Rd., 3 miles west of US-23, Howell. (517) 546-3211.
One par 5 followed by a 266-yard, par 3.
Par 35, 3392 yards. Range $

MARION OAKS (18)
2255 Pinckney Rd., 1-1/2 miles south of I-96 Exit 137, Howell. (517) 548-0050.
Opened mid-season 1990. Salem Hills' Godwin family owns it and son Frank worked on construction and shaping after Harry Bowers (The Rock) routed it. Wildflowers planted between fairways. Gently rolling, some woods, some wetlands.
Par 70, 6175 yards. S108. *$$ [bar, grill]*

OAK POINTE GOLF CLUB (36)
5341 Brighton Rd., Brighton. (313) 227-4541.
There are three different looks at the former Burroughs Farms. Upscale (and price) is the nine-hole Honors Course (par 36, 3488 yards) designed by Art Hills with a second nine under construction. It's big league. Old style is the ego-builder Championship Course at 5998 yards, par 71 and then there's the even shorter nine hole Challenge Course at 1241 yards and par 27. They've added a practice range and food is top drawer and medium priced in Roadhouse restaurant.
Championship S107, Honors S132. Range *$$ & $$$ [restaurant]*

RUSH LAKE HILLS GOLF CLUB (18)
3199 Rush Lake Rd., north of M-36, Pinckney. (313) 878-9790.
Par 73, 6500 yards. *$ [bar, grill]*

TYRONE HILLS (18)
8449 US-23, Center Rd. Exit 75, Fenton. (313) 629-5011.
The real Hills of Tyrone are in Northern Ireland but these will do for Livingston County. Another nicely-maintained, enjoyable course by Bruce Matthews.
Par 72, 6300 yards. S121. *$$ [bar, grill]*

WOODLAND GOLF CLUB (18)
7635 Grand River, Brighton. (313) 229-9663.
Saw a bluebird there and must be the bluebird of happiness as owners are improving the 5015-yard, par 67 course. It's short —four par 4s under 300 yards — but not a push-over.
$

MONROE COUNTY

CARLETON GLEN GOLF CLUB (18)
13470 Grafton Rd., west of I-275 Exit 8, Carleton. (313) 654-6201.
Friendly place and it's become a favorite for golf-loving Japanese employees at the Flat Rock Mazda plant.
Par 71, 3130 yards. $$ [bar, grill]

CHERRYWOOD GOLF CLUB (9)
7910 Whiteford Center Rd., Ottawa Lake. (313) 856-6669.
Won't wear you out.
Par 35, 3000 yards. $

DEME ACRES GOLF COURSE (18)
17655 Albain Rd., 1 mile east of Petersburg. (313) 279-1151.
Price is right — low end of scale. Three par 4s under 300 yards produce birdies.
Par 70, 5735 yards. $

DUNDEE GOLF CLUB (9)
13851 S. Custer Rd., Dundee. (313) 529-2321.
Comfortable yardages — longest par 4 is 365 and two bunkerless par 5s are 500 and 535.
Par 36, 3050 yards. $ [grill]

GREEN MEADOWS GOLF COURSE (18)
1555 Strasburg Rd., Monroe. (313) 242-5566.
Par 70, 6400 yards. $ [bar, grill]

GIANT OAK GOLF CLUB (18)
1024 Valetta Dr., Temperance. (313) 847-6733.
Early Arthur Hills design. Name comes from 300-year-old oak between first green and second tee. It was growing before Cadillac sailed the Detroit River. Trunk diameter is 10 feet plus. Championship course is par 72, 6600 yards and executive course is par 29, 1464 yards. $ [bar, grill, banquet facilities]

LILAC BROTHERS GOLF COURSE (18)
9090 Armstrong Rd., I-75 Exit 21 east, Newport. (313) 586-9902.
Par 72, 7052 yards. $ [bar, grill]

RAISIN RIVER GOLF CLUB (36)
1500 N. Dixie Hwy., I-75 Exit 15 east Monroe. (313) 289-3700.
Flat but nicely maintained and ponds and creek in play on both sides.
East course par 71, 6930 yards, West course par 68, 6240 yards. Range *$$ [bar, grill]*

THORNE HILLS GOLF COURSE (9)
12915 Sumpter Rd., west of Carleton. (313) 587-2332.
Holes fair length for 3035-yard, par 36 — one par 4 under 300 yards.
$ [bar, grill]

WESBURN GOLF COURSE (18)
5617 S. Huron River Dr., South Rockwood. (313) 379-3555.
Par 72, 6200 yards. *$*

WHITEFORD VALLEY GOLF COURSE (36)
8440 Old US-223, Ottawa Lake. (313) 856-4545.
One is par 71, 6500 yards; other is par 72, 6900 yards. *$ [bar]*

$ — Greens fee to $15
$$ — Greens fee to $25
$$$ — Greens fee to $50
$$$$ — Greens fee more than $50
Range — Driving range available
S — Slope rating

SOUTH CENTRAL MICHIGAN

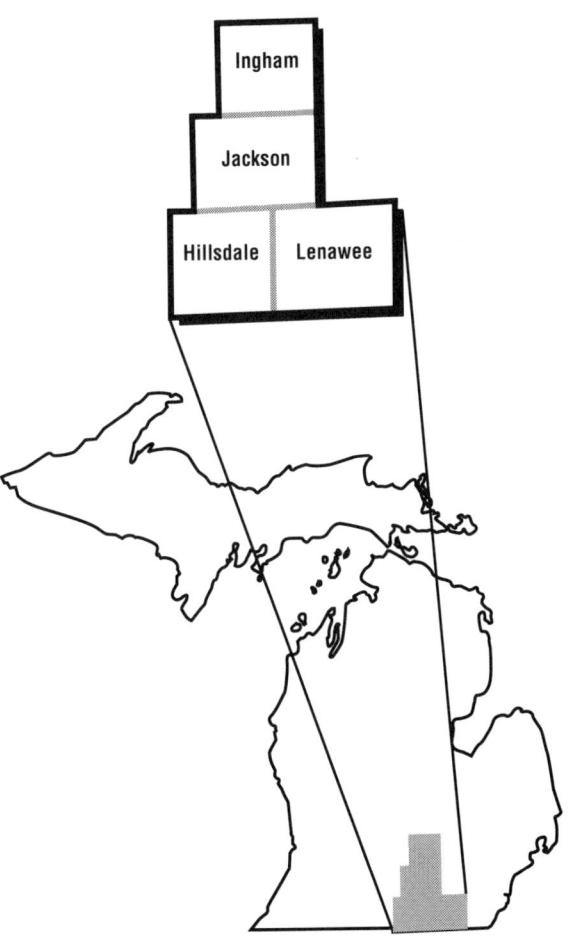

HILLSDALE COUNTY

JENKINS PUBLIC GOLF COURSE (9)
1001 Homer Rd., Litchfield. (517) 542-3121.
Par 36, 3200 yards. *$ [bar, grill]*

LAKE LeANN GOLF COURSE (9)
10399 Fairway Blvd., Somerset Center. (517) 688-3445.
Par 35, 2850 yards. Range *$ [bar, grill]*

MILL RACE GOLF COURSE (9)
200 Adrian Rd., Jonesville. (517) 849-9439.
Narrow, heavily treed.
Par 36, 3150 yards. S126. Range *$*

WHITE OAKS GOLF COURSE (9)
2171 Bankers Rd., Hillsdale. (517) 437-3434.
Par 34, 2650 yards. $ [bar, grill]

INGHAM COUNTY

BRANSON BAY GOLF COURSE (18)
215 Branson Bay Dr., Mason. (517) 663-4144.
Relatively tight, second nine added several years ago and very challenging.
Par 72, 6111 yards. *$ [bar, grill]*

BROOKSHIRE INN & GOLF COURSE (9)
205 W. Church St., Williamston. (517) 655-4694.
Short but tight with an excellent long par 3 through a chute of trees.
Par 35, 2900 yards. *$ [restaurant]*

CHISHOLM HILLS GOLF COURSE (18)
2397 S. Washington Rd., Lansing. (517) 694-0169.
Ego-ville. Wide open, short, good condition.
Par 70, 5700 yards. S95. *$ [bar, grill]*

EL DORADO COUNTRY CLUB (18)
3750 W. Howell Rd., Mason. (517) 676-2854.
Par 72, 6659 yards. Range *$ [bar, grill, banquet facilities, catering]*

FOREST AKERS GOLF COURSE (36)
Harrison Rd. at Mt. Hope, East Lansing. (517) 355-1635.
Michigan State University's courses designed by alumnus Bruce Matthews who got his bachelor's in landscape architecture in 1925. Telephone in advance. Par 71, 6750-yard West Course is tougher of the pair with Slope of 119. Nice mix of holes and rolling. East course is 6510 yards, par 71. S112. Range $$ *[snacks]*

FOUR WINDS GOLF COURSE (9)
5850 Park Lake Rd., East Lansing. (517) 339-1500.
Par 35, 3000 yards. Range $ *[restaurant]*

GROESBECK GOLF COURSE (18)
1600 Ormond Rd., Lansing. (517) 483-4333.
Excellent Lansing muny with good mix: six tough, six semi-tough and six easy. Governor Alexander Groesbeck dedicated it with the first shot in 1926. Par 72, 6200 yards. S118. $ *[beer, sandwiches]*

INDIAN HILLS GOLF COURSE (9)
4811 Nakoma Dr., Okemos. (517) 349-1010.
On the banks of the Red Cedar.
Par 33, 2700 yards. $

LAKE O' THE HILLS GOLF COURSE (9)
2101 Lac Du Mont, Haslett. (517) 339-9445.
A nice Bruce and Jerry Matthews course. Walkers only, apartment complex.
Par 3, 1362 yards. $

MASON HILLS GOLF CLUB (18)
2602 Tomlinson, Mason. (517) 676-5366.
Second nine added length and woods.
Par 72, 6500 yards. Range $ *[grill, snacks, restaurant]*

OAK LANE GOLF COURSE (18)
4875 N. Main, Webberville. (517) 521-3900.
Not tough but well-conditioned and popular.
Par 70, 6000 yards. $ *[bar, grill]*

PINE LAKE GOLF COURSE (18)
1018 Haslett Rd., Haslett. (517) 339-8281.
Well-treed, overlooks Lake Lansing.
Par 71, 6026 yards. $ *[bar, grill]*

THE PLAYERS CLUB GOLF COURSE (9)
925 S. Canal Rd., Lansing. (517) 627-8687.
No connection with PGA Tour Players Clubs which are name designer monster tracks. This one is 3100 yards, par 35. $

RED CEDAR GOLF COURSE (9)
203 S. Clippert, Lansing. (517) 351-3254.
Short muny.
Par 34, 2600 yards. $ *[sandwiches]*

ROYAL SCOT GOLF & BOWL (18)
4722 W. Grand River, Lansing. (517) 321-6220.
Between the airport and a cemetery. Wide open, interesting greens.
Par 71, 6600 yards. S109. Range $ *[bar, grill]*

SYCAMORE GOLF COURSE (9)
1526 E. Mt. Hope, Lansing. (517) 482-1890.
Ego course, short muny with five par 4s and four 3s. A little tight.
Par 33, 2343 yards. $ *[sandwiches]*

TIMBER RIDGE GOLF COURSE (18)
16339 Park Lake Rd., East Lansing. (517) 339-8000.
You'd swear you were in northern Michigan. May be Jerry Matthews' best work and was ranked among three best new public courses in America by *Golf Digest* when it opened in 1989. Nice flow to it and they work on conditioning.
Par 72, 6500 yards. S128. Range $$$ *[bar, grill]*

WAVERLY HILLS GOLF COURSE (9)
3619 W. Saginaw, at Waverly Rd., Lansing.
(517) 323-1986.
Long par 36, 3377 yard muny with a 600-yard, par 5.
$ *[sandwiches]*

WILLOW CREEK GOLF CLUB (9)
3252 Heeney Rd., Stockbridge. (517) 851-7856.
Par 35, 2850 yards. Range $ *[bar, grill]*

JACKSON COUNTY

BURR OAK GOLF COURSE (18)
3491 N. Parma Rd., Parma. (517) 531-4741.
Very good condition. Pair of back-to-back par 3s that measure close to 200 yards.
Par 72, 6300 yards. Range $ *[bar, grill]*

CASCADES GOLF COURSE (18)
1992 Warren Ave., Jackson. (517) 788-4323.
County operates it and layout and care are evidence of why Jackson produces so many championship players. Just a fine golf course. Starts with pair of par 5s, first is downhill and second returns uphill.
Par 72, 6614 yards. S120. Range $ *[snacks]*

CLARK LAKE GOLF COURSE (27)
5535 Wesch Rd., Brooklyn. (517) 592-6259.
Big course is par 72, 7000 yards and other nine is par 34, 3000 yards. Original nine short, up and down and fun. New 18 needs some maturity.
Range $ *[bar, grill, banquet facilities]*

CONCORD HILLS GOLF COURSE (18)
7331 Pulaski Rd., Concord. (517) 524-8337.
Fine championship course.
Par 72, 6500 yards. Range $ *[bar, sandwiches]*

DEER RUN GOLF CLUB (9)
3200 Hanover Rd., north of US-12, Horton.
(517) 688-3350.
Par 36, 3200 yards. $ *[bar, grill]*

ELLA SHARP PARK GOLF COURSE (18)
2880 S. 4th Street, Jackson. (517) 788-4066.
City course which, like county's Cascades, is well-run and maintained.
Par 71, 6000 yards. $

GAUSS' GREEN VALLEY GOLF COURSE (18)
5751 Brooklyn Rd., Jackson. (517) 764-0270.
Par 70, 6035 yards. Range $ *[bar, grill]*

GRACEWIL PINES GOLF COURSE (18)
5400 Trailer Park Dr., Jackson. (517) 764-4200.
Par 72, 6300 yards. $ *[bar, grill]*

GREENBRIAR (18)
14820 Wellwood Rd., Brooklyn. (517) 592-6952.
Short stuff.
Par 66, 5000 yards. $

HANKARD HILLS GOLF COURSE (9)
10251 Resort Rd., east of US-127, Pleasant Lake.
(517) 769-2507.
Par 34, 2600 yards. $ *[bar, grill]*

HICKORY HILLS GOLF COURSE (18)
2540 Par View Dr., Jackson. (517) 750-3636.
Give it a C plus to a B.
Par 72, 6400 yards. Range $ [bar, grill]

HILL'S HEART OF THE LAKES (9)
500 Case Rd., Brooklyn. (517) 592-2110.
Senior PGA Tour star Mike Hill and his family own and operate it. Mike's done so well on Old Boy circuit that he's in process of adding second nine to the par 34, 2600-yard original nine. Jeff Gorney did new nine which was scheduled for spring seeding.
$ [bar, grill]

LAKELAND HILLS GOLF COURSE & LOUNGE (18)
5119 Page Ave., Jackson. (517) 764-5292.
First to open, last to close — great drainage.
Par 72, 6070 yards. S108. $

SPARROW HAWK GOLF COURSE (9)
2618 Seymour Rd., Jackson. (517) 787-1366.
Next to I-94, Exit 141. Looks tougher from the highway with those pine-lined holes than it really is.
Par 36, 3100 yards. Range $ [snacks]

TWIN KNOLLS GOLF COURSE (9)
10400 Mack Island Rd., Grass Lake. (517) 522-8944.
Poorly designed greens keep good golfers away. Par 36, 3005 yards. $ [bar, sandwiches]

WATERLOO GOLF COURSE (9)
11800 Trist Rd., Grass Lake. (517) 522-8527.
Par 35, 2800 yards. S105. Range $ [grill]

WHIFFLETREE HILL GOLF COURSE (18)
15730 Homer, Concord. (517) 524-6655.
Former dairy farm became a golf course in 1969. Front nine is open, back nine through woods.
Par 70, 6000 yards. Range $ [bar, grill]

LENAWEE COUNTY

CENTERVIEW (18)
5640 N. Adrian Hwy., M-52, Adrian.
(517) 263-8081.
Flat, good length, lot of trees and lot of play.
Par 71, 6800 yards. *$ [snacks]*

DeMOR HILLS GOLF COURSE (18)
10275 Ranger Hwy., Morenci. (517) 458-6697.
Short stuff — driveable par 4s.
Par 72, 6340 yards. *$ [bar, grill, restaurant]*

DEVIL'S LAKE GOLF COURSE (9)
14600 US-223, Manitou Beach. (517) 547-3653.
Location, location, location. In heart of Devil's Lake vacation area known as Little Ohio and the Buckeyes keep ringing that cash register.
Par 36, 3100 yards. Range *$*

EVERGREEN GOLF COURSE (9)
16124 Cadmus, Hudson. (517) 448-8017.
Not a bad little par 36, 2800 yards. *$ [snacks]*

MACON GOLF CLUB (9)
11064 Macon Hwy., Clinton. (517) 423-4259.
Nice, par 35, 3000 yards. *$ [bar, grill]*

RAISIN VALLEY GOLF CLUB (18)
4057 Comfort Rd., Tecumseh. (517) 423-2050.
Nice and a little hilly, between Tecumseh and Adrian.
Par 72, 5800 yards. *$ [bar, grill]*

SILVER LAKE GOLF COURSE (9)
15649 US-12, Brooklyn. (517) 592-8036.
Par 3, 1275 yards. Range *$*

WOODLAWN GOLF CLUB (18)
4634 Treat Hwy., Adrian. (517) 263-3288.
Busy, always nice condition and striving to improve.
Par 72, 6000 yards. *$ [bar, grill]*

SOUTHWEST MICHIGAN

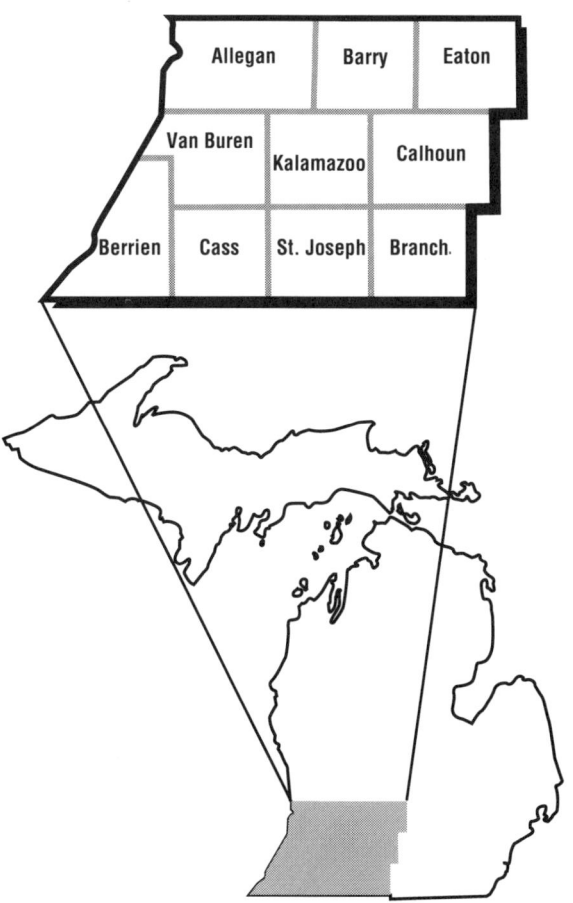

ALLEGAN COUNTY

CHESHIRE HILLS GOLF COURSE (18)
102nd Ave., Allegan. (616) 673-2882.
Not long but some unique holes and adding nine more.
Par 70, 5727 yards. S109. Range $ *[bar, grill]*

CLEARBROOK GOLF CLUB (18)
135th Ave., Saugatuck. (616) 857-1766.
Not long but has trees and water.
Par 72, 6447 yards. S120. Range $$ *[bar, grill]*

GLENN SHORES GOLF CLUB (9)
111th Ave., Blue Star Hwy., South Haven. (616) 227-3226.
Short one near the big lake.
Par 30, 2940 yards. $ *[snacks]*

HIDDEN VALLEY GOLF COURSE (18)
1069 126th Ave., Shelbyville. (616) 672-7866.
Par 60, 3530 yards. $ *[grill, restaurant]*

LAKE DOSTER GOLF CLUB (18)
136 Country Club Blvd., Plainwell. (616) 685-5308.
Charlie Scott, son of Gull Lake View complex owner Darl Scott, designed Lake Doster which has been regarded as one of southwest Michigan's best since it opened in 1967. Par 3 third hole is only 101 yards but it's The Little Monster with Lake Doster's arms around it, front and back.
Par 72, 6570 yards. S125. Range $$ *[bar, restaurant]*

LAKE MONTEREY GOLF COURSE (18)
2814 Fairway, Dorr. (616) 896-8118.
Nine executive holes and nine nice regular holes.
Par 65, 4712 yards. $ *[grill]*

MI-RO GOLF COURSE (9)
396 Chase Rd., 1 mile south of Saugatuck, Douglas. (616) 857-2271.
Flat and fast and by the big lake.
Par 36, 3700 yards. Range $

ORCHARD HILLS GOLF COURSE (27)
714 125th Ave., Shelbyville. (616) 672-7096.
Flat, farmland course in Yankee Springs State Park area. Popular for outings.
Par 72, 6135 yards. S122. Range *$ [bar, grill, snacks, sandwiches]*

OT-WELL-EGAN COUNTRY CLUB (9)
1058 Lincoln Rd., Allegan. (616) 673-8261.
Older course, small greens, well-kept.
Par 36, 3310 yards. S114. *$ [restaurant]*

PRAIRIEWOOD GOLF COURSE (18)
315 Prairiewood Dr., 2 miles west of M-131, Otsego. (616) 694-6633.
At time of publication, new nine still scheduled to open in 1991.
Par 72, 6500 yards. *$*

SOUTH HAVEN GOLF CLUB (18)
Blue Star Memorial Hwy., South Haven. (616) 637-3896.
Nice. Used to be private club and it shows.
Par 72, 6400 yards. Range *$ [bar, sandwiches]*

WESTSHORE GOLF CLUB (18)
14 Ferry St., Douglas. (616) 857-2500.
More short stuff.
Par 66, 5300 yards. S105. *$*

WINDING CREEK GOLF COURSE (18)
8600 Ottogan St., Holland. (616) 396-4516.
And that creek does wind through it. Challenging.
Par 72, 6700 yards. S118. Range *$$ [snacks]*

BARRY COUNTY

GUN RIDGE GOLF COURSE (9)
4460 Gun Lake Rd., Hastings. (616) 948-8366.
Nice executive.
Par 35, 2420 yards. *$$*

MULBERRY FORE GOLF COURSE (18)
955 N. Main, Nashville. (517) 852-0760.
Par 72, 6000 yards. *$ [bar, grill]*

MULLENHURST GOLF COURSE (18)
9810 Mullen Rd., Delton. (616) 623-8383.
Short but scenic, fun and little jewel at par 71, 5625 yards. *$ [snacks]*

RIVER BEND GOLF COURSE (27)
1370 W. State Rd., Hastings. (616) 945-3238.
Short course but nice. Hosts big fall scramble each year.
Par 72, 5000 yards. Range *$ [bar, snacks]*

YANKEE SPRINGS GOLF COURSE (27)
12300 Bowens Mill Rd., Wayland. (616) 795-9047.
Popular with summer cottagers. Nines of 3200 (par 36), 3100 (par 36) and 2800 (par 35) yards. *$ [bar, restaurant]*

BERRIEN COUNTY

BLOSSOM TRAILS GOLF COURSE (27)
1565 E. Britain Rd., Benton Harbor. (616) 925-4951.
One of Bruce Matthews' early works in Michigan's fruitland. Also a 9-hole par 3.
Par 70, 6100 yards. S117. *$ [bar, restaurant]*

BROOKWOOD GOLF COURSE (18)
1339 Rynearson Rd., Buchanan. (616) 695-7818.
New owners have improved it; well-conditioned.
Par 72, 6800 yards. Range *$ [bar, grill]*

GRAND BEACH GOLF COURSE (9)
48200 Perkins Blvd., Grand Beach, New Buffalo. (616) 469-4888.
Par 36, 2830 yards. *$ [grill]*

INDIAN LAKE HILLS GOLF COURSE (18)
55321 Brush Lake Rd., Eau Claire. (616) 782-2540.
Well-kept par 71, 6200 yards. *$ [bar, grill]*

LAKE MICHIGAN HILLS GOLF CLUB (18)
2520 Kerlikowske, Benton Harbor. (616) 849-2722.
Good course, up and down, lot of trees and used as qualifying course for Western Amateur.
Par 72, 6914 yards. S129. Range *$$ [bar, restaurant, banquet facilities]*

THE OAKS GOLF CLUB (18)
3711 Niles Rd., St. Joseph. (616) 429-8411.
Nice.
Par 72, 6914 yards. Range $$ *[bar, grill]*

PAW PAW LAKE GOLF CLUB (18)
4548 Forest Beach Rd., Watervliet. (616) 463-3831.
Driveable par 4s.
Par 70, 5457 yards. Range $ *[bar, outdoor BBQ]*

PEBBLEWOOD GOLF COURSE (18)
9794 Jericho Rd., Bridgman. (616) 465-5611.
Ego builder.
Par 68, 5400 yards. $ *[restaurant, banquet facilities]*

PIPESTONE CREEK (18)
6768 Naomi Rd., 1-1/2 mile west of M-140, Eau Claire. (616) 944-1611.
Par 67, 4400 yards. $ *[bar, sandwiches]*

PLYM PARK GOLF COURSE (9)
401 Marmont, Niles. (616) 684-7331.
Muny, decent condition, busy. Carts prohibited.
Par 35, 3100 yards. $ *[bar, snacks, sandwiches]*

BRANCH COUNTY

BRONSON GOLF COURSE (9)
1015 Brink Rd., Bronson. (517) 369-6745.
Unremarkable.
Par 36, 3260 yards. $ *[bar]*

IYOPAWA ISLAND GOLF COURSE (9)
13004 Iyopawa Island, Coldwater. (517) 238-2216.
Executive.
Par 36, 2900 yards. $

QUINCY GOLF COURSE (9)
60 Miller Rd., Quincy. (517) 639-4491.
Gets a grade of 'C.'
Par 34, 2757 yards. S119. $ *[bar, snacks]*

CALHOUN COUNTY

ALWYN DOWNS (18)
1225 S. Kalamazoo, 1 mile south of Fountain Circle, Marshall. (616) 781-3905.
Straightforward and right price.
Par 70, 6500 yards. *$ [bar, sandwiches]*

BEDFORD VALLEY GOLF COURSE (18)
23161 Waubascon Rd., Battle Creek. (616) 965-3384.
Good, solid par 72, 6890-yard course with bracing set of par 3s. Hosted Michigan Open 1970-77 and is one of Michigan's best. Owned by Darl Scott family and that's a mark of excellence.
S127. Range *$$ [bar, grill]*

BINDER PARK GOLF COURSE (18)
6723 B Drive South, Battle Creek. (616) 966-3459.
Charlie Scott designed it, nice course with a lot of trees. They're looking to add another nine.
Par 71, 6350 yards. *$ [beer & wine]*

CEDAR CREEK GOLF CLUB (18)
14000 Renton Rd., Battle Creek. (616) 965-6423.
A 'C' for CC.
Par 72, 6225 yards. *$ [bar, snacks, sandwiches]*

MARYWOOD GOLF CLUB (18)
21310 North Ave., Battle Creek. (616) 968-1168.
Used to be a private club and the par 72, 6842-yard layout has all the touches including lavish flowers. One of state's best greens fee buys.
S125. Range *$$$ [bar, grill, restaurant]*

OAKLAND HILLS GOLF CLUB (18)
11619 H Drive North, Battle Creek. (616) 965-0809.
No, not THE Oakland Hills but this one is public.
Par 72, 6630 yards. *$*

SPRINGBROOK (9)
1600 Avenue A, Springfield. (616) 964-9313.
Par 36, 3300 yards. *$*

TOMAC WOODS GOLF COURSE (18)
14827 26-1/2 Mile Rd., Albion. (517) 629-8241.
Well, price is right.
Par 72, 6290 yards. Range *$ [bar, snacks]*

TURTLE CREEK GOLF CLUB (18)
9044 R Drive South, Burlington. (517) 765-2232.
Another 'C' for this ego builder.
Par 70, 5230 yards. S104. *$ [bar, grill]*

CASS COUNTY

BRYN MAWR GOLF CLUB (18)
26831 Dutch Settlement Rd., Dowagiac. (616) 782-5827.
Owned by Chicagoans and better than average.
Par 71, 6300 yards. S116. Range *$$ [bar, restaurant]*

DIAMOND LAKE GOLF CLUB (9)
22041 Golf Lane, Cassopolis. (616) 445-3143.
Par 35, 2700 yards. *$*

DOWAGIAC ELKS GOLF COURSE (9)
Riverside Dr. to Underwood Dr., Dowagiac. (616) 782-5685.
Short.
Par 36, 3110 yards. *$*

GARVER LAKE GOLF COURSE (9)
25320 May St., Edwardsburg. (616) 663-6463.
Shorter.
Par 34, 2700 yards. *$ [snacks]*

HAMPSHIRE COUNTRY CLUB (18)
29592 Pokagon Highway, Dowagiac. (616) 782-7476.
Fact that it is one of the qualifying sites for the Western Amateur makes it special. Designed by Chicagoan Lawrence Packard, it is the best public course in the county and at a nice price.
Par 72, 7000 yards. S118. *$ [bar, snacks, sandwiches]*

PARK SHORE GOLF COURSE (9)
610 Park Shore Dr., Cassopolis. (616) 445-2834.
Unremarkable.
Par 35, 3100 yards. *$*

EATON COUNTY

BONNIE VIEW GOLF COURSE (9)
311 Michigan Rd. (M-99), Eaton Rapids. (517) 663-4363.
Nice name.
Par 36, 3139 yards. $

BUTTERNUT BROOK GOLF COURSE (18)
2200 Island Hwy., Charlotte. (517) 543-0570.
Grade it 'C.'
Par 71, 6289 yards. Range $ *[snacks]*

CENTENNIAL ACRES GOLF COURSE (18)
12485 Dow Rd., Sunfield. (517) 566-8055.
Warner Bowen, who did Schuss Mountain, did this.
Par 72, 6650 yards. $ *[bar, grill]*

GRAND LEDGE COUNTRY CLUB (18)
5811 St. Joe Hwy., Grand Ledge. (517) 627-2495.
Well-conditioned and pulls a grade of 'B.'
Par 72, 6170 yards. S114. $ *[snacks]*

LEDGE MEADOWS GOLF COURSE (18)
1801 Grand Ledge Hwy., Grand Ledge. (517) 627-7492.
Par 72, 6392 yards. S113. Range $ *[bar, grill]*

OLIVET COUNTRY CLUB (9)
6819 Old US-27, Olivet. (616) 749-9051.
Comfortable 'C.'
Par 36, 3000 yards. $ *[bar, grill]*

KALAMAZOO COUNTY

CRESTVIEW (18)
900 West D Ave., Kalamazoo. (616) 349-1111.
Short, popular.
Par 70, 6010 yards. S100. $

EASTERN HILLS GOLF CLUB (27)
6075 East G Ave., Kalamazoo. (616) 385-8175.
Very busy — 57,000 yearly rounds. The 18-holer is spacious and one nine is through trees and with some water. Good condition. Two nines of 3300 yards, one of 3100.
All par 36. White/Blue S112, White/Red S113, Blue/Red S114. $ *[snacks]*

GRAND PRAIRIE (9)
3620 Grand Prairie Rd., Kalamazoo. (616) 388-4447.
Forget the 1 iron.
Par 30, 1720 yards. $

GULL LAKE VIEW GOLF CLUB (36)
7417 N. 38th St., Augusta. (616) 731-4148.
West is oldest and longest at 6200 yards (par 71) open on front and back is rolling with water on six holes. East is par 70 and 5700 yards with smaller greens, well-bunkered and water on 11 of the 18 holes. Owned and operated by Darl Scott family which owns Stonehedge and Bedford Valley a little farther east. Scott brand translates to quality golf and conditions. Rolling terrain. Some rental units on premises and popular weekend spot for foursomes. E&W S120. $$ *[bar, grill]*

INDIAN RUN GOLF CLUB (18)
6359 East RS Ave., Portage. (616) 327-1327.
Good condition, nice course.
Par 72, 7000 yards. Range $ *[bar, restaurant]*

MAPLE HILLS GOLF CLUB (9)
16344 C Ave. East, 1 mile north of M-89, Augusta. (616) 731-4430.
Par 35, 2950 yards. S110. Range $ *[bar]*

MILHAM PARK GOLF COURSE (18)
4200 Lovers Lane, Kalamazoo. (616) 344-7639.
Good, strong municipal course, lot of bunkers and trees, rolling terrain and no carts which helps maintain fine condition — never any ground under repair here.
Par 72, 6500 yards. S118. Range $ *[snacks]*

OAKLAND HILLS GOLF COURSE (9)
8716 Oakland Dr., Portage. (616) 327-1493.
Popular with seniors, good beginner course.
Par 35, 3000 yards. Range $ *[snacks]*

OLDE MILL GOLF CLUB (18)
6101 West XY Ave., Schoolcraft. (616) 679-5625.
Heavy play and you get some run in dry weather.
Par 72, 6565 yards. S114. Range $ *[bar, grill]*

RIDGE VIEW GOLF COURSE (18)
10360 W. Main St., Kalamazoo. (616) 375-8821.
Always open unless it's under snow.
Par 71, 6600 yards. *$ [bar, grill]*

STATES GOLF COURSE (18)
20 East W Ave., Ave., Vicksburg. (616) 649-1931.
Heavy play, open, not challenging.
Par 72, 6250 yards. *$ [bar, grill]*

STONEHEDGE GOLF COURSE (18)
M-89, Augusta. (616) 731-2300.
Terrifically enjoyable course with northern Michigan flavor in southern Michigan. Owned by Darl Scott family which also owns Gull Lake View and Bedford Valley. Son Charlie designed it and it's a course you want to go back to. Aptly named — lot of stone hedges on the property from long-ago farm days.
Par 72, 6600 yards. S124. Range *$$ [bar, grill]*

THORNAPPLE CREEK GOLF CLUB (18)
6415 West F Ave., Kalamazoo. (616) 344-0040.
The 593-yard 13th (550 from middle) hole is reminiscent of the famed 13th at the Dunes Club in Myrtle Beach, designed by Robert Trent Jones. Lake is all around the right side and has to be carried eventually.
Par 72, 6800 yards. S125. *$$ [bar, grill]*

ST. JOSEPH COUNTY

GREEN VALLEY GOLF & HEALTH CLUB (18)
25379 Fawn River Rd., Sturgis. (616) 651-6331.
Executive.
Par 68, 5615 yards. *$ [bar, grill]*

PINE VIEW GOLF CLUB (36)
52065 Pulver Rd., Three Rivers. (616) 279-5131.
Two well-maintained courses of 6400 and 6700 yards owned and operated by Greg Matthews, one of most inspiring men in Michigan sport. Lost his eyesight but not his vision and runs strong hands-on operation.
Par 72. Hemlock S111, Spruce S119. Range *$$ [bar, grill]*

ST. JOE VALLEY GOLF CLUB (18)
24953 M-86, Sturgis. (616) 467-6275.
Short but above average.
Par 68, 5200 yards. S107. *$ [bar, grill]*

SAUGANUSH COUNTRY CLUB (18)
61270 Lutz Rd., Three Rivers. (616) 278-7825.
Older course, short, some unique holes, elevated greens.
Par 72, 5780 yards. *$ [bar, grill]*

VAN BUREN COUNTY

JEPTHA LAKE GOLF COURSE (9)
20551 47th St., Bloomingdale. (616) 427-9910.
Par 3, 1100 yards. *$ [bar, snacks]*

LAKE CORA HILLS GOLF CLUB (18)
671 County Rd., 4 miles west of Paw Paw. (616) 657-4074.
In lake district, owned by top Kalamazoo amateur Bert Cooper. Fun course, undulating greens.
Par 72, 6150 yards. *$ [bar, grill]*

MARKS GOLF (9)
N. Main St., Lawton. (616) 624-2051.
Par 35, 2957 yards. Range *$*

SHAMROCK HILLS GOLF COURSE (18)
31071 County Road 390, Gobles. (616) 628-2070.
Par 66, 5200 yards. Range *$ [bar, grill]*

$ — Greens fee to $15
$$ — Greens fee to $25
$$$ — Greens fee to $50
$$$$ — Greens fee more than $50
Range — Driving range available
S — Slope rating

MIDDLE MICHIGAN EAST

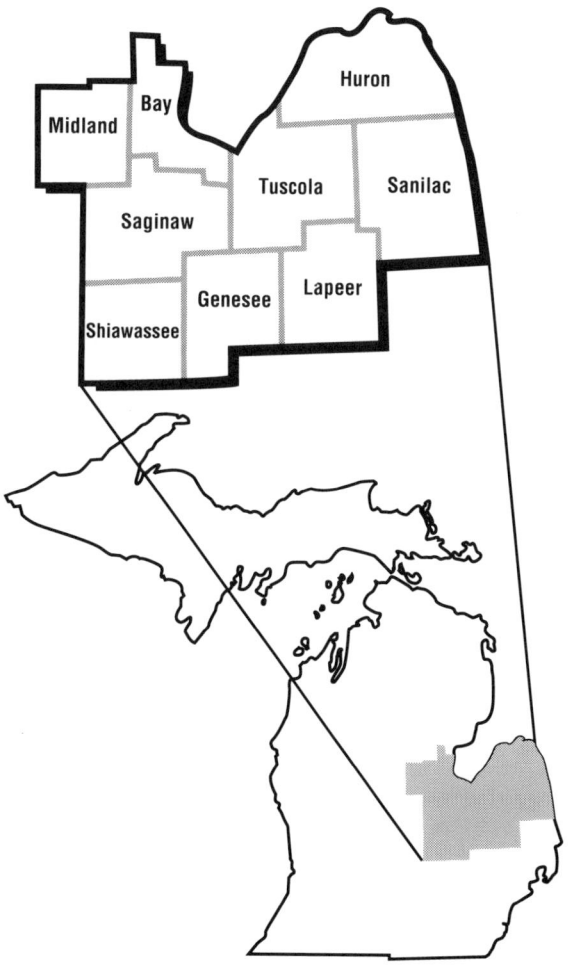

BAY COUNTY

BAY COUNTY GOLF COURSE (18)
584 W. Hampton Rd., Essexville. (517) 892-2161.
Conditioning is strong point of popular county-operated course. Par 72, 6550 yards. S107. Range *$
[snacks]*

BAY VALLEY GOLF CLUB (18)
2470 Old Bridge Rd., Exit 160 off I-75, Bay City. (517) 686-5400.
Desmond Muirhead did it. Desmond Who? Well, he mentored Jack Nicklaus through Muirfield Village. Signature hole is the par 3 165-yard 14th, the Heather Hole. If you make it over the stuff to the green, it's heather; if you're in it, they're weeds. Fun course with good location for southeast Michiganians who want to get away for a couple of days but don't want to drive all the way north. Carts required.
Par 71, 6610 yards. S121. Range *$$$ [bar, restaurant]*

GREEN HILLS GOLF COURSE (18)
1699 North M-13, Pinconning. (517) 697-3011.
Short and popular.
Par 71, 5800 yards. *$ [bar, grill]*

MAPLE LEAF GOLF COURSE (18)
158 N. Mackinaw, Linwood. (517) 697-3531.
Par 70, 6015 yards. *$ [bar, grill]*

SANDY RIDGE GOLF COURSE (18)
2750 W. Lauria Rd., Midland. (517) 631-6010.
Par 72, 6250 yards. S117. *$ [bar, grill]*

SPRING VALLEY GOLF CLUB (9)
2635 E. Beaver Rd., Kawkawlin. (517) 686-0330.
Par 36, 3342 yards. *$*

TWIN OAKS GOLF COURSE (27)
6710 Freeland Rd., Freeland. (517) 695-9746.
Nines of 2755 (par 35), 2810 (par 36) and 3020 (par 36) yards. *$*

WHITE BIRCH HILLS GOLF COURSE (18)
360 Ott Rd., Bay City. (517) 662-6523.
Bruce Matthews designed it. Next to Tri-City Speedway so get a move on.
Par 70, 5225 yards. *$ [bar, grill]*

GENESEE COUNTY

BEECHWOOD GREENS GOLF COURSE (9)
1161 W. Frances Rd., Mt. Morris. (313) 686-4200.
Short stuff.
Par 32, 2045 yards. Range $

GENESEE VALLEY MEADOWS (18)
5499 Miller Rd., Swartz Creek. (313) 732-1401.
Once a private club, still retains those touches. Popular, well-kept course.
Par 72, 6772 yards. S127. $$ [bar, grill]

GOODRICH COUNTRY CLUB (18)
10080 Hegel Rd., Goodrich. (313) 636-2493.
Tricky, and bumps in the greens make putting a challenge.
Par 70, 5460 yards. S104. $$ [bar, grill]

GRAND BLANC COUNTRY CLUB (27)
5270 Perry Rd., Grand Blanc. (313) 694-5960.
Larry Mancour designed strong third nine which regulars call "Troon." Fine conditioning.
Par 72, 6545 yards. S108. Range $$ [bar, grill, banquet facilities]

KEARSLEY LAKE GOLF COURSE (18)
4266 E. Pierson, Flint. (313) 736-0930.
Best of city's munys.
Par 72, 6520 yards. $

KING PAR GOLF & DRIVING RANGE (9)
65140 Flushing Rd., 1-1/2 miles west of I-75, Flushing. (313) 732-2470.
Adjacent nine-hole natural grass pitching wedge course is domed in winter and called Winter Greens (313) 230-1966.
Par 3, 800 yards. Range $

LOCH LOMOND GOLF COURSE (9)
5267 S. Dort Hwy., Flint. (313) 742-1434.
Nice short course.
Par 34, 2600 yards. S102. Range $ [bar, grill]

MOTT PARK GOLF COURSE (9)
2401 Nolan Dr., Flint. (313) 766-7077.
Muny. Walkers only.
Par 36, 2942 yards. $

PIERCE PARK GOLF COURSE (18)
2302 Brookside Dr., at Court & Dort Hwy., Flint. (313) 766-7297.
Popular with juniors and seniors.
Par 3, 2300 yards. $ [grill]

RIVER FOREST GOLF COURSE (9)
3571 Rue Fort, at Beecher Rd. & I-75, Flint. (313) 732-9240.
One of best-viewed courses in the state — it's on the east side of busy I-75.
Par 3, 1100 yards. $

SOUTHMOOR GOLF COURSE (18)
G-4312 S. Dort Hwy., Burton. (313) 743-4080.
Still another Matthews course and nicely kept.
Par 70, 5300 yards. Range $ [bar, grill]

SWARTZ CREEK GOLF COURSE (27)
1902 Hammerberg, Flint. (313) 766-7043.
Muny with 6748-yard, par 72 18-hole course and additional executive nine, 3342-yard, par 36.
$ [bar, vending machines only]

TORREY PINES GOLF CLUB (18)
12312 Torrey Rd, east side of US-23, Fenton. (313) 629-1212.
Older course and lots of roll on the summer fairways.
Par 72, 6200 yards. $ [bar, snacks]

VIENNA GREENS GOLF COURSE (18)
1184 E. Tobias Rd., Clio. (313) 686-1443.
Par 70, 6335 yards. S108. $ [bar, grill]

WILLOWBROOK PUBLIC GOLF COURSE (18)
311 W. Maple, Byron. (313) 266-4660.
Par 72, 6305 yards. S115. $ [bar, grill]

WINTER GREENS GOLF CLUB (9)
Flushing Rd., 1-1/2 miles west of I-75, Flushing. (313) 230-1966.
Par 3, 800-yard course is covered by translucent dome in winter. $

HURON COUNTY

BIRD CREEK GOLF CLUB (18)
M-53, 1 mile south of Port Austin. (517) 738-4653.
New Jerry Matthews design.
Par 72, 6200 yards. Range $$

CASEVILLE GOLF COURSE (9)
5848 Griggs Rd., Caseville. (517) 856-2613.
Short and quick.
Par 35, 2810 yards. Range $ *[snacks]*

CENTURY OAKS GOLF COURSE (9)
4570 M-142, Elkton. (517) 375-4419.
Short but not necessarily easy.
Par 35, 2965 yards. S113. Range $ *[snacks, beer & wine]*

SCENIC GOLF & COUNTRY CLUB (18)
M-25, bet. Bayport & Caseville, Pigeon. (517) 453-3350.
Par 72, 6034 yards. S114. Range $$ *[bar, grill]*

VERONA HILLS GOLF CLUB (18)
3175 Sand Beach Rd., Bad Axe. (517) 269-8132.
Long regarded as best public course in the Thumb and it actually has hills!
Par 71, 6500 yards. S125. Range $$ *[bar, grill]*

LAPEER COUNTY

ARCADIA HILLS GOLF COURSE (9)
3801 Haines Rd., Attica. (313) 724-6967.
Par 36, 2700 yards. $ *[bar, sandwiches]*

GREENBRIER GOLF COURSE (18)
9350 N. Lapeer Rd., Mayville. (517) 843-6575.
Par 71, 5700 yards. $ *[bar, grill]*

HADLEY ACRES GOLF COURSE (9)
3797 S. Hadley, Hadley. (313) 797-4820.
Par 36, 3250 yards. $ *[bar, grill, restaurant]*

LAPEER COUNTRY CLUB (18)
3786 Hunt Rd., Lapeer. (313) 664-2442.
Par 72, 6000 yards. S114. $ *[bar, grill, restaurant]*

Middle Michigan East

LUM INTERNATIONAL GOLF COURSE (27)
5191 Lum Rd., Lum. (313) 724-0851.
New 3200-yard, par 35 nine opens this year.
Par 72, 6000 yards. Range *$ [bar]*

ROLLING HILLS GOLF CLUB (18)
3274 Davidson, Lapeer. (313) 664-2281.
Par 71, 6480 yards. S113. Range *$ [bar, grill]*

WASHAKIE GOLF & RV RESORT (18)
3461 Burnside Rd., North Branch. (313) 688-3235.
One hundred on-premise modern campsites.
Par 72, 5755 yards. *$ [snacks]*

MIDLAND COUNTY

CURRIE GOLF COURSE (36)
1006 Currie Parkway, Midland. (517) 839-9600.
Well-kept municipal operation has 6400-yard, par 72
18-holer plus two nines of 3200 yards, par 36, and
1000 yards, par 27.
East S119. Range *$ [snacks]*

SAGINAW COUNTY

BEECH HOLLOW GOLF COURSE (18)
7494 Hospital Rd., Freeland. (517) 695-5427.
Short, easy scoring.
Par 72, 5931 yards. *$ [bar, grill]*

COUNTRY CLUB OF REESE (9)
2280 S. Reese Rd., Reese. (517) 868-4991.
Par 35, 3100 yards. Range *$ [bar, grill]*

CROOKED CREEK GOLF COURSE (18)
9387 Gratiot Rd., Saginaw. (517) 781-0050.
Popular with seniors and leagues.
Par 72, 6000 yards. Range *$ [snacks]*

FRANKENMUTH GOLF CLUB (18)
950 Flint St., Frankenmuth. (517) 652-9229.
Closed this year while remodeling original nine and
adding a second nine. But there's still plenty of
chicken and mashed potatoes and gravy.

GREEN ACRES GOLF COURSE (18)
7323 Dixie Hwy., Bridgeport. (517) 777-3510.
One of county's better courses, wooded, some tight driving holes and difficult greens.
Par 72, 6238 yards. S115. Range $ *[bar, grill]*

KIMBERLEY OAKS GOLF CLUB (18)
1100 W. Walnut, St. Charles. (517) 865-8261.
Pricey but best in Saginaw area. Hosts many outings. Carts required.
Par 72, 6700 yards. S123. Range $$$ *[bar, grill]*

PLEASANT VIEW GOLF COURSE (9)
3424 Barnard Rd., Saginaw. (517) 791-4768.
Unremarkable.
Par 35, 2800 yards. Range $ *[snacks]*

SWAN VALLEY GOLF COURSE (18)
9499 Geddes Rd., Saginaw. (517) 781-4945.
Quite good.
Par 70, 6400 yards. $ *[bar, grill]*

TWIN BROOKS GOLF CLUB (18)
1005 McKeighan Rd., Chesaning. (517) 845-6403.
New second nine strengthens course.
Par 72, 6411 yards. S119. Range $ *[bar, grill]*

VALLEY VIEW FARMS GOLF COURSE (18)
1435 S. Thomas Rd., Saginaw. (517) 781-1248.
Well-conditioned.
Par 71, 6252 yards. S112. $

SANILAC COUNTY

E.M.S. LINKS GOLF COURSE (9)
2236 S. Isles Rd., Sandusky. (313) 648-2256.
Three ponds and drainage ditch that runs across four holes grab some balls.
Par 36, 2850 yards. $ *[bar, snacks]*

HURON SHORES GOLF CLUB (9)
1441 N. Lakeshore, Port Sanilac. (313) 622-9961.
Par 35, 2600 yards. $ *[bar, grill]*

LAKEVIEW HILLS GOLF COURSE (36)
M-90, 1-1/2 miles west of Lexington. (313) 359-7333.
Original nine holes designed by Walter Hagen opened in 1935, hilly with Lake Huron views. Second nine added in 1950. New 18 begun by Bill Newcomb and finished by Jeff Gornley, woods, island green, Lake Huron views. Some accommodations. Original course par 72, 6200 yards; new course par 72, 6800 yards.
Range $$ *[bar, grill, banquet facilities]*

MARLETTE COUNTRY CLUB (9)
2701 Golf Course Rd., Marlette. (517) 635-3009.
Par 36, 2900 yards. S109. Range $ *[snacks]*

WILLOW TREE GOLF & COUNTRY CLUB (9)
232 Galbraithline, Melvin. (313) 387-9898.
Par 36, 3000 yards. Range $ *[bar, grill]*

WOODLAND HILLS GOLF COURSE (18)
430 Stoney Creek Dr., Sandusky. (313) 648-2400.
Couple long, tough par 3s.
Par 72, 6576 yards. S115. Range $ *[bar, grill]*

SHIAWASSEE COUNTY

BRAD VAN PELT'S GOLF COURSE (9)
4377 S. M-52, Owosso. (517) 725-9194.
Who was Owosso's Most Famous Son, Tom Dewey or Brad Van Pelt? Both got their men, Dewey as a New York D.A. and Van Pelt as an All-American D.B. at Michigan State and later the New York Giants. But did Dewey play golf?
Par 36, 3023 yards. Range $ *[bar, grill]*

CHIPPEWA HILL COUNTRY CLUB (9)
5300 Bancroft, Durand. (517) 743-3277.
Par 35, 3000 yards. Range $ *[bar, grill]*

CORUNNA HILLS GOLF COURSE (9)
on Legion Rd., Corunna. (517) 743-4693.
Par 36, 3000 yards. $ *[bar, grill]*

DUTCH HOLLOW GOLF CLUB (18)
8500 E. Lansing Rd., Durand. (517) 288-3960.
Par 71, 5700 yards. $ *[bar, grill]*

GLENBRIER GOLF COURSE (18)
4178 Locke Rd., south of I-69, Perry. (517) 625-3800.
Par 71, 6000 yards. $ *[bar, grill]*

PINE HILLS GOLF COURSE (9)
6603 N. Woodbury, Laingsburg. (517) 651-7781.
Par 35, 2351 yards. $ *[snacks]*

TUSCOLA COUNTY

ARROWHEAD GOLF & COUNTRY CLUB (9)
1201 Gun Club Rd., Caro. (517) 673-2017.
Par 36, 2800 yards. $ *[bar, grill, restaurant]*

CARO GOLF CLUB (9)
1080 E. Caro Rd., Caro. (517) 673-7797.
Par 35, 2900 yards. $ *[bar, grill]*

ROLLING HILLS GOLF COURSE (9)
6586 E. Milligan, Cass City. (517) 872-3569.
Better than average.
Par 35, 2900 yards. S105. Range $ *[bar, grill]*

SHERWOOD ON THE HILL (9)
6625 Third St., Gagetown. (517) 665-9971.
Par 34, 2500 yards. $ *[bar, grill]*

VASSAR GOLF & COUNTRY CLUB (18)
3509 Kirk Rd., Vassar. (517) 823-7221.
Best in the county, on the flat side, not great but nice.
Par 72, 6440 yards. S116. $ *[bar, grill]*

WILLOW SPRINGS GOLF & COUNTRY CLUB (18)
7335 Oak Rd., Vassar. (517) 871-9703.
Par 68, 4639 yards should mean low scores. Two nines: Regulation, par 36, 2871 yards; Executive, par 32, 1768 yards. $

MIDDLE MICHIGAN WEST

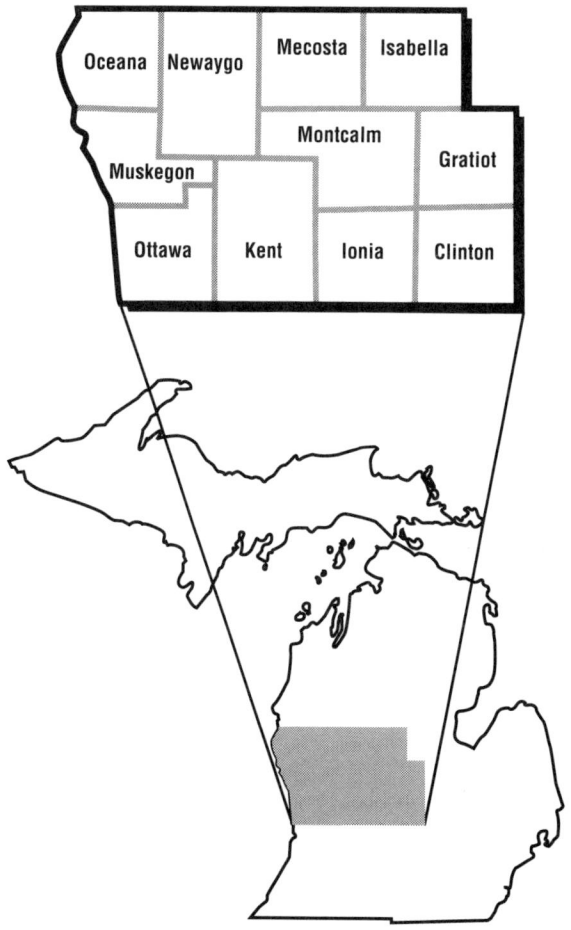

CLINTON COUNTY

CHARDELL GOLF COURSE (9)
4646 Howe Rd., Bath. (517) 641-4123.
Unremarkable.
Par 35, 3100 yards. Range $ *[bar, snacks]*

CLINTON COUNTY COUNTRY CLUB (9)
8103 N. US-27. St. Johns. (517) 224-6287.
Well-kept.
Par 35, 2900 yards. Range $ *[bar, grill]*

HIGHLAND HILLS GOLF CLUB (18)
450 E. Alward, DeWitt. (517) 669-9873.
Above average.
Par 72, 6700 yards. Range $ *[bar, grill, banquet facilities]*

PRAIRIE CREEK GOLF COURSE (18)
800 E. Webb, DeWitt. (517) 669-3091.
Short stuff.
Par 70, 6075 yards. $ *[bar, grill]*

TWIN OAKS GOLF COURSE (9)
6345 N. US-27, St. Johns. (517) 224-7342.
Par 36, 3200 yards. $ *[bar, grill]*

GRATIOT COUNTY

EDGEWOOD HILLS COUNTRY CLUB (9)
1270 W. Monroe Rd., St. Louis. (517) 681-3404.
Nice.
Par 36, 3200 yards. Range $ *[bar]*

GRATIOT COUNTRY CLUB (9)
1508 N. State Rd., Ithaca. (517) 875-4612.
Par 35, 3500 yards. $

NORTH STAR GOLF COURSE (18)
4550 S. Bagley Rd., Ithaca. (517) 875-3841.
The manager is Tuff Rummer. Honest.
Par 70, 5800 yards. S105. $ *[bar, grill]*

OVERBROOK (9)
6234 W. Grant, Middleton. (517) 236-5357.
Par 35, 3020 yards. $ *[bar, hot dogs]*

IONIA COUNTY

CANDLESTONE INN & GOLF RESORT (18)
8100 N. Storey Rd., Belding. (616) 794-1580.
Jerry Matthews considers it one of his best "least-known" courses. Nice little getaway spot with accommodations. Home of West Michigan Amateur.
Par 72, 6630 yards. S125. Range $$ *[restaurant, 24 room inn]*

MORRISON LAKE COUNTRY CLUB (18)
6425 Portland Rd., Saranac. (616) 642-9528.
Better than average.
Par 70, 5555 yards. S101. $ *[bar, grill]*

PORTLAND COUNTRY CLUB (18)
Divine Hwy., Portland. (517) 647-4521.
Check the slope rating for short course.
Par 70, 5600 yards. S114. $ *[bar, restaurant]*

RIDGEVIEW GOLF CLUB (9)
5200 Flat River Trail, Belding. (616) 794-1860.
How short is short?
Par 35, 2225 yards. $ *[snacks]*

ISABELLA COUNTY

HOLIDAY GREENS (18)
5665 E. Picard at M-20 and US-27, Mt. Pleasant. (517) 772-2905.
Good spot to do some ironing. Nine par 4s, nine par 3s. Well-conditioned.
Par 63, 3700 yards. $ *[Holiday Inn behind has pool, restaurant, bar, & grill]*

PLEASANT HILLS GOLF COURSE (18)
4452 E. Millbrook, Mt. Pleasant. (517) 772-0487.
Ego-builder with short par 4s.
Par 71, 6100 yards. Range $ *[bar, grill]*

THE PINES GOLF COURSE OF LAKE ISABELLA (18)
7231 Club House Dr., Weidman. (517) 644-2300.
Owners reversed Horace Greeley's advice and came east for fame and fortune. Or, at least to buy a golf course in Michigan after sizing up opportunities in Rocky Mountain states and California. The Pines hosted eight Michigan Public Links state championships and the par 72, 6800-yarder gets more difficult as pines fill out.
S120. Range $ *[restaurant]*

RIVERWOOD GOLF CLUB (27)
1239 E. Broomfield, Mt. Pleasant. (517) 772-5726.
PGA Tour star Dan Pohl played here as youngster and so did LPGA's Cindy Figg-Currier whose parents, Dick and Betty Figg, own the course. Figgs host annual junior tournament which is one of best in the state. Nines of 2232 (par 34), 2963 (par 36) and 3186 (par 36) yards with woods, water and length. Challenging.
Slope Red/White 121, Red/Blue 109, White/Blue 111. Range $$

VALLEY VIEW GOLF CLUB (18)
8240 Genuine Rd., Shepard. (517) 828-6618.
Wide open spaces.
Par 72, 6800 yards. Range $ *[bar, grill, banquet facilities]*

KENT COUNTY

ALPINE GOLF CLUB (18)
6320 Alpine Ave. NW, Comstock Park. (616) 784-1064.
One of Mark De Vries' early courses. Open, parallel fairways, juniors and seniors, well-conditioned.
Par 72, 6201 yards. S119. $$ *[bar, grill]*

ARROWHEAD GOLF COURSE (18)
2170 Alden Nash NE, Lowell. (616) 897-7264.
Well, green grass releases oxygen, doesn't it?
Par 72, 6262 yards. $ *[bar, grill]*

Jack Berry's Guide to Michigan Golf

BRAYSIDE, THE GOLF CLUB AT COURTLAND HILLS (18)
5460 11 Mile Rd., Rockford. (616) 866-1402.
Relatively new Mark De Vries design still in maturing stage. Greens undulating and a challenge.
Par 71, 6800 yards. $ *[bar, grill]*

BRIARWOOD GOLF CLUB (18)
2900 92nd St., Caledonia. (616) 698-8720.
Open and popular with juniors and beginners. New nine opening late summer.
Par 72, 6052 yards. Range $ *[bar, restaurant]*

BROADMOOR COUNTRY CLUB (18)
7725 Kraft, Caledonia. (616) 891-8000.
Bit more challenging, got some length and popular with leagues.
Par 72, 6500 yards. Range $ *[bar, grill]*

BYRON HILLS GOLF COURSE (27)
7330 Burlingame, Byron Center. (616) 878-1522.
Price is right.
Par 72, 6300 yards, other nine par 34, 2500 yards. $

DEER RUN GOLF CLUB (18)
13955 Cascade, Lowell. (616) 897-8481.
Michigan Publinx championship played here in early 80s. Long and challenging, finishes with two par 5s. Play it when it's dry.
Par 72, 6900 yards. S123. Range $ *[bar, grill]*

ENGLISH HILLS GOLF COURSE (18)
1200 Four Mile Rd., Grand Rapids. (616) 784-3420.
Ego-builder.
Par 69, 5495 yards. $ *[bar, grill]*

GRACEWIL COUNTRY CLUB (36)
2597 Four Mile Rd., Walker exit of I-96, Grand Rapids. (616) 784-2455.
Both courses built in 1928 and set among apple orchards. Very pretty in the spring.
Both par 72, 6300 yards. $ *[bar, grill]*

GRAND ISLAND GOLF RANCH (18)
6266 West River Dr., Belmont. (616) 363-1262.
Wide open but don't play it when the Grand River is up.
Par 72, 6266 yards. Range $ *[snacks]*

GRAND RAPIDS GOLF CLUB (27)
4300 Leonard NE, Grand Rapids. (616) 949-2820.
Open, hosts many outings.
Par 71, 6400 yards and nine of par 35, 3000 yards.
Range $ *[bar, snacks]*

INDIAN TRAILS GOLF COURSE (18)
2776 Kalamazoo Ave. SE, Grand Rapids. (616) 245-2021.
Grand Rapids muny alongside busy 28th Street so plenty of "Fores!" from passing bozos.
Par 68, 5089 yards. $

IRONWOOD GOLF COURSE (18)
3750 64th St., Byron Center. (616) 538-4000.
Lots of irons on this shorty but not many woods.
Par 71, 5400 yards. $ *[beer]*

L.E. KAUFMAN GOLF COURSE (18)
4829 Clyde Park, Wyoming. (616) 538-5050.
Grand Rapids' best muny. Got a new super and conditioning has improved. When conditioned properly it's among five best in west Michigan. Strong finishing holes on each nine.
Par 72, 6700 yards. S121. Range $ *[snacks]*

LINCOLN COUNTRY CLUB (18)
3485 Lake Michigan Dr. NW, Grand Rapids. (616) 453-6348.
Unremarkable.
Par 72, 6200 yards. S110. $ *[bar, grill]*

MAPLE HILL GOLF COURSE (18)
5555 Ivanrest, Grandville. (616) 538-0290.
Exceptionally well-maintained executive course with good range attached.
Par 68, 4500 yards. S112. Range $ *[beer]*

MEADOWLANE GOLF COURSE (18)
3356 44th St. SE, Kentwood. (616) 698-8034.
Price right for beginners.
Par 72, 5800 yards. Range $ *[bar, snacks]*

NORTH KENT GOLF COURSE (18)
11029 Stout Ave. NE, Rockford. (616) 866-2659.
Nicely maintained, exceptionally fast greens for public course.
Par 70, 6400 yards. Range $ *[bar, grill]*

THE PINES GOLF COURSE (18)
5050 Byron Center Ave. SW, Wyoming. (616) 538-8380.
Good scrambles course for mid to high handicappers. An ego-builder.
Par 70, 6800 yards. Range $ *[snacks, sandwiches]*

ROGUE RIVER GOLF COURSE (18)
12994 Paine Ave. NW, Sparta. (616) 887-7182.
Warner Bowen course is short but pretty.
Par 70, 5670 yards. $ *[bar, grill]*

SASKATOON GOLF CLUB (27)
9038 92nd St., Alto. (616) 891-8652.
West Michigander Mark De Vries designed it and it's among his best and among five best public courses in West Michigan. Former home of Grand Rapids Match Play Championship. Very popular and adding fourth nine which should open this fall. Has woods, water and length on present 27.
Par 35, 3011 yards; par 36, 3220 yards; par 37, 3522 yards. Range $ *[bar, restaurant]*

SCOTT LAKE COUNTRY CLUB (18)
911 Hayes NE, Comstock Park. (616) 784-1355.
Friendly folks and well-maintained.
Par 72, 6300 yards. Range $ *[bar, snacks]*

TYLER CREEK GOLF COURSE (18)
13495 92nd St. SE, Alto. (616) 868-6751.
You can whack an electrifying shot on the 190-yard 18th. A Consumers Power pole is in the back left corner of the putting surface — honest — 10 feet in from the fringe. The course owner was going to have Consumers take it out but when he found out how much it would cost, he left it in. A Mark De Vries design.
Par 70, 6175 yards. $

MECOSTA COUNTY

KATKE GOLF COURSE (18)
Ferris State University, Big Rapids. (616) 592-3765.
Well-conditioned — students in Professional Golf Management course learn the ropes here. Challenging with several very strong par 3s.
Par 72, 6600 yards. S118. Range $$ *[restaurant]*

WINTERS CREEK GOLF COURSE (18)
13120 Northland Dr., Big Rapids. (616) 796-2613.
Nice, no crusher.
Par 72, 6200 yards. S113. Range $$ *[bar, grill, restaurant, banquet facilities]*

MONTCALM COUNTY

BIRCHWOOD GOLF COURSE (9)
6900 Masters Rd., Howard City. (616) 762-4424.
Par 36, 2954 yards. $ *[grill]*

BROOKSIDE GOLF COURSE (9)
1518 Johnson Rd., Gowen. (616) 984-2381.
Average.
Par 35, 3100 yards. Range $ *[bar, grill]*

CRYSTAL GOLF COURSE (18)
2122 Straight Tow Blvd., Crystal. (517) 235-6616.
Short and shorter.
One nine is par 35, 2800 yards and other nine is a par 3 of 1200 yards. $

EDMORE GOLF COURSE (9)
615 W. Home, Edmore. (517) 427-3241.
Par 36, 3000 yards. $

HOLLAND LAKE GOLF COURSE (9)
1100 E. Holland Lake Rd., Sheridan. (517) 291-5757.
Warner Bowen design, rolling, wooded, eight water holes.
Par 36, 3140 yards. $ *[bar, grill]*

WHITEFISH LAKE GOLF CLUB (9)
2241 Bass Lake Rd., Pierson. (616) 636-5260.
Popular with summer cottagers.
Par 36, 3045 yards. Range $

MUSKEGON COUNTY

BENT PINE GOLF CLUB (18)
2480 Duck Lake Rd. Whitehall. (616) 766-2045.
Par 72, 6100 yards. $ *[bar, grill]*

CHASE HAMMOND GOLF COURSE (18)
2454 N. Putnam Rd., Muskegon. (616) 766-3035.
Muskegon County's answer to Grand Haven just down the coast. Mark De Vries, active West Michigan designer and Michigan State alumnus, did it in 1969.
Par 72, 6400 yards. Range *$ [bar]*

FRUITPORT COUNTRY CLUB (18)
6330 S. Harvey, Muskegon. (616) 798-3355.
Not long, not well-known but those who know it love it.
Par 71, 5725 yards. *$ [bar, grill]*

HICKORY KNOLL GOLF COURSE (27)
3065 W. Alice St., Whitehall. (616) 894-5535.
A step back in time in price and feel. Very popular with seniors. Three par 35 nines of 2800, 3000 and 3100 yards. *$*

LINCOLN GOLF CLUB (18)
4907 N. Whitehall Rd., Muskegon. (616) 766-3636.
Once a private club and continues the tradition of fine conditioning and good greens. A keeper.
Par 72, 6100 yards. S117. Range *$ [bar, grill]*

OAK RIDGE GOLF CLUB (18)
513 Pontaluna Rd, Muskegon. (616) 798-3660.
Next to Hoffmaster State Park.
Par 72, 6158 yards. S123. Range *$$ [bar, grill, banquet facilities]*

OLD CHANNEL TRAIL GOLF COURSE (18)
Rt. 3, Old Channel Trail, Montague. (616) 894-5076.
The original nine was designed by Chicagoan Robert Bruce Harris, co-founder and first president of the American Society of Golf course architects. Later Bruce Matthews added a second nine and in the process, two of the original holes were eliminated so Matthews actually did 11 holes. Deep bunkers plus Lake Michigan breezes toughen the par 71, 6166-yarder. Golf pro Jack Bendelow is grandson of Scots-born Tom Bendelow who laid out the first municipal golf course in the United States — Van Cortlandt Park in the Bronx.
$ [bar, sandwiches, picnic area]

PARKVIEW GOLF COURSE (18)
4600 S. Sheridan Dr., Muskegon. (616) 773-8814.
Par 3, 2000 yards. $

RAVENNA GOLF COURSE (18)
11566 Heights of Ravenna Rd., Ravenna. (616) 853-6736.
Par 72, 6137 yards. $

UNIVERSITY PARK GOLF COURSE (9)
2100 Marquette, Muskegon. (616) 773-0023.
Par 36, 3100 yards. Range $

NEWAGO COUNTY

BRIAR HILL GOLF COURSE (18)
950 W. 40th, Fremont. (616) 924-2070.
Average.
Par 72, 6000 yards. $ *[bar, grill]*

BRIGADOON GOLF CLUB (18)
12559 Bagley, Grant. (616) 834-8200.
Dentist Grant McKinley following his dental dad's footsteps — his father built Pine Valley in Macomb County. McKinley laid out and bull-dozed this himself and there's plenty of blind shots, water and bunkers. Some call it bizarre and say take every old ball you own.
Par 72, 6162 yards. S131. Range $$

NORTHWOOD GOLF COURSE (18)
288 Comstock, Fremont. (616) 924-3380.
Average.
Par 71, 6252 yards. Range $ *[snacks]*

VILLAGE GREEN GOLF CLUB (9)
8130 Bingham, Newaygo. (616) 652-6513.
More short stuff.
Par 34, 2800 yards. S106. Range $ *[bar, restaurant]*

OCEANA COUNTY

BENONA SHORES GOLF COURSE (18)
3410 Scenic Dr., Shelby. (616) 861-2098.
Warner Bowen did this short course between Silver and Stony lakes and near the big lake in 1979 and proved short can be good.
Par 60, 4200 yards. *$ [snacks]*

OCEANA COUNTRY CLUB (18)
3333 W. Weaver Rd., Shelby. (616) 861-4211.
Good scenic par 73, 6100 yards. S114. *$ [snacks]*

OTTAWA COUNTY

CRESTVIEW GOLF CLUB (18)
6279 96th Ave., Zeeland. (616) 875-8101.
Fast track.
Par 72, 6097 yards. S101. *$ [grill, banquet facilities]*

FAIRWAY GOLF CLUB (27)
6150 14th Ave., Hudsonville. (616) 457-3680.
Flat and fast. Nines of 2800 (par 34), 3000 (par 36) and 2950 (par 36) yards. *$*

GRAND HAVEN GOLF CLUB (18)
17000 Lincoln Rd., Grand Haven. (616) 842-4040.
Bruce Matthews' pride and joy. Grand Old Man of Michigan designers owns the course and lives on it so conditioning always is top-notch. Been rated in *Golf Digest's* Best Public Courses in America. Take your straight game or you'll be knocking pines all day. Tight with capital "T."
Par 72, 6800 yards. S119. Range *$$ [snacks]*

HOLLAND COUNTRY CLUB (18)
51 Country Club Rd., Holland. (616) 392-1844.
No windmills but creek meanders through.
Par 70, 6000 yards. S109. Range *$$*

LIL ACRES GOLF COURSE (9)
1831 Johnson, Marne. (616) 677-3379.
Name says it all: par 30, 1800 yards. *$*

SUMMERGREEN GOLF COURSE (9)
3441 New Holland, Hudsonville. (616) 669-0950.
Short stuff.
Par 30, 2000 yards. *$*

TERRA VERDE GOLF CLUB (18)
11741 W. Leonard Rd., Nunica. (616) 837-8249.
Rolling, ponds and creeks. Bruce and Jerry Matthews collaboration.
Par 70, 6000 yards. *$ [bar, restaurant, banquet facilities]*

WESTERN GREENS COUNTRY CLUB (18)
2475 Johnson St., Marne. (616) 677-3677.
Moderately difficult course designed by Mark De Vries and rates are right.
Par 71, 6500 yards. Range *$ [bar, grill]*

WEST OTTAWA GOLF COURSE (27)
6045 136th St., Holland. (616) 399-1678.
Sruba family runs good operation.
Par 70, 6200 yards and additional nine of par 35, 2800 yards. Range *$*

$ — Greens fee to $15
$$ — Greens fee to $25
$$$ — Greens fee to $50
$$$$ — Greens fee more than $50
Range — Driving range available
S — Slope rating

NORTHEAST MICHIGAN

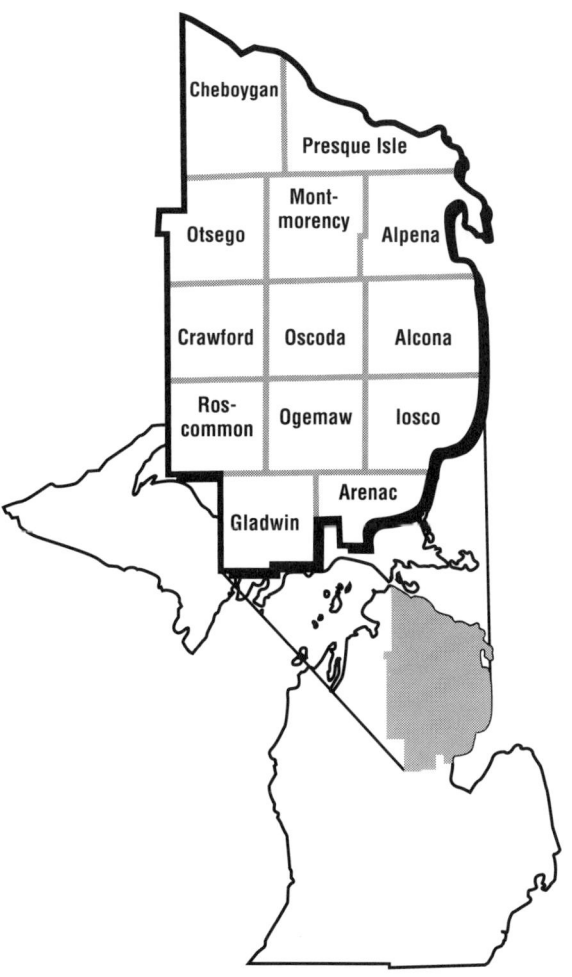

ALCONA COUNTY

GREENBUSH GOLF COURSE (9)
1981 US-23, Greenbush. (517) 724-6356.
The nine-holer was built in 1927 by Carl Schmidt who introduced the sugar beet to Michigan, according to current Greenbush owner Ben Walker. Walker has planted 2800 Lombardy poplars and says the course is "like an extension of my back yard." Sporty par 36, 3080 yards and a very good restaurant.
$ [bar, grill]

SPRINGPORT HILLS GOLF COURSE (9)
5184 E. Springport Rd., Harrisville. (517) 724-5611.
Wide open and hilly. Owner Steve Ashford putting everything back into course and nice restaurant. Par 36, 2900 yards. S108. *$ [restaurant, no liquor]*

ALPENA COUNTY

ALPENA GOLF CLUB (18)
1135 Golf Course Rd., Alpena. (517) 354-5052.
Designed by Warner Bowen. They're good holes. Back side is 3100 yards from the middle tees compared to 2900 on the front.
Par 72, 5986 yards. Range *$$ [snacks]*

ARENAC COUNTY

HURON BREEZE GOLF & COUNTRY CLUB (18)
5200 Huron Breeze Dr., just off US-23, 4-1/2 miles north of Au Gres. (517) 876-6868.
First nine opened in 1988 and second nine opens this year. Bill Newcomb designed it among the birches and in the sand just a stout par 5 in from Lake Huron. Been a lot of sweat equity by the member-owners who got down and dirty including laying irrigation pipe. A good-looking course.
Par 72, 6838 yards. Range *$$ [bar, grill]*

PINE RIVER GOLF CLUB (9)
2244 Pine River Rd., Standish. (517) 846-6819.
Par 36, 3310 yards. S121. Range *$ [bar, grill]*

CHEBOYGAN COUNTY

CHEBOYGAN GOLF & COUNTRY CLUB (18)
1431 Old Mackinaw Rd., 1-1/2 miles west of Cheboygan. (616) 627-4264.
Undergoing half million dollar remodeling.
Par 70, 6004 yards. Range $$ [bar, grill]

INDIAN RIVER GOLF CLUB (18)
6460 Chippewa Beach Rd., Indian River. (616) 238-7011.
Regarded as one of the best secrets in the north for playability and price.
Par 72, 6700 yards. S118. $$ [grill]

MULLETT LAKE COUNTRY CLUB (9)
Mullett Lake. (616) 627-5971.
No pushover.
Par 36, 3282 yards. S117. $

CRAWFORD COUNTY

FOX RUN COUNTRY CLUB (18)
5825 W. Four Mile Rd., just west of I-75, Exit 251, Grayling. (517) 348-4343.
Designed by Jeff Gorney and opened last year. Managing partner Jerry DeWitt anxious to please. Fun layout and friendly folks. Par 4 fourth only 377 yards from the back, 332 from the middle but the sharp dogleg left is No. 1 handicap hole. It will slow play until players figure it out. And there are indeed animal dens — DeWitt said 52 have been counted.
Par 72, 6160 yards. S123. Range $$ [bar, grill]

GRAYLING COUNTRY CLUB (18)
M-72, Grayling. (517) 348-5618.
Just added second nine by Jeff Gorney. Flat, 5707 yards (par 70).
S112. Range $$ [bar, grill]

GLADWIN COUNTY

GLADWIN HEIGHTS GOLF COURSE (18)
3551 W. M-61, Gladwin. (517) 426-9941.
Par 71, 6110 yards. S110. Range $ [bar, grill]

SUGAR SPRINGS COUNTRY CLUB (18)
1930 W. Sugar River Rd., Gladwin. (517) 426-4391.
Jerry Matthews designed it. Course never has made big push for northbound golf business.
Par 72, 6737 yards. S119. Range *$$ [bar, grill]*

IOSCO COUNTY

LAKEWOOD SHORES RESORT (18)
7751 Cedar Lake Rd., Oscoda. (517) 739-2075.
Jerry Matthews designed it and even though it's flat as a pancake, it's the best course on northeast quarter of the Lower Peninsula. It's been underplayed because of lower traffic volume to Sunrise Side. Stan Aldridge, owner of Indianwood Golf & Country Club in Lake Orion, owns Lakewood Shores and plans two more courses designed by Bob Cupp who did the New Course at Indianwood, restored the Old Course and had considerable input on The Bear at Grand Traverse when he was chief designer for Jack Nicklaus. Par 72, 6528 yards. S117. Range *$$ [bar, grill, restaurant]*

TAWAS GOLF COURSE (18)
1022 Monument Rd., Tawas. (517) 362-6262.
Play increasing steadily as owners Steve and Peg Sonoga make improvements and golf traffic increases around the very pleasant Tawases. They've put in bunkers and some small ponds but Sonoga isn't creating a monster. It's a playable par 72, 6505 yards.
$ [bar, restaurant]

WICKER HILLS COUNTRY CLUB (9)
5 miles north of Hale off M-65, Hale. (517) 728-9971.
Par 36, 3005 yards. Range *$$ [bar, sandwiches]*

MONTMORENCY COUNTY

ELK RIDGE GOLF COURSE (18)
5 miles north of Atlanta, west of M-33, Atlanta. (517) 785-4683 or (800) 626-4ELK.
Opens this year. Designed by Jerry Matthews for Honeybaked Hams owner Lou Schmidt. Yes, Honeybaked ham will be served in the clubhouse. Wonderful views and topography, specimen 100-foot white and red pines. Take your camera. Also golf balls because the wetland cross hazards on 17 and 18 are going to gobble a bunch. As for the elk — two bulls tore up the first green October, 1990.
Par 72, 6800 yards. Range $$$ *[bar, grill]*

THUNDER BAY GOLF COURSE (18)
M-32, east of Hillman. (517) 742-4875.
Owner Jack Matthias, sparkplug of Sunrise Side Golf, added second nine last year and it's a much more difficult hazardous side at 2822 yards and par 38 to the front's 3103 yards and par 37. Matthias and his wife, Jan, and manager Gene LaFramboise designed it and superintendent Chuck Schaudt did the work to keep price down. Incidentally, this is the Thunder Bay River, not the bay on Lake Huron by Alpena — that's 20 miles east.
Par 73, 6466 yards. S129. $$$ *[bar, grill, restaurant]*

OGEMAW COUNTY

CRAPO HILLS GOLF COURSE (9)
2100 Maes, West Branch. (517) 345-2971.
Par 35, 2700 yards. $

EDGEWOOD FOREST GOLF COURSE (9)
2160 Sage Lake Rd., 4 miles north of Prescott off M-55, Prescott. (517) 873-5427.
Par 35, 2500 yards. $ *[snacks]*

WEST BRANCH COUNTRY CLUB (18)
198 Fairview Rd., West Branch. (517) 345-2501.
Par 72, 6400 yards. S116. Range $$ *[bar, grill]*

OSCODA COUNTY

CEDAR VALLEY GOLF CLUB (9)
3757 Weaver Rd., Comins. (517) 848-2792.
Par 36, 3000 yards. *$*

FAIRVIEW HILLS GOLF CLUB (9)
1481 N. Caldwell Rd., Mio. (517) 848-5810.
Par 36, 3180 yards. *$ [snacks]*

GARLAND RESORT (63)
County Road 489, Lewiston. (517) 786-2211.
Most one-stop golf in Michigan with three 18s — Monarch, Swampfire and Reflections — plus Herman's Nine (par 36, 3224 yards), the original walking nine. Lots of water in play on 6056-yard Monarch and 5937-yard Swampfire. Water in view but not in play so much on Reflections which starts with several holes funneled through tall pines. Owner Ron Otto did the designing himself. Beautiful property, lots of wildlife — deer, turkey — and excellent accommodations. Superb craftsmanship in wood carvings and stained glass windows in main lodge. Also have packages on corporate jet that lands on Garland airstrip. Cart required.
Monarch: par 72, 6056 yards; Swampfire: par 72, 5937 yards; Reflections: par 72, 5966 yards. Monarch S130, Swampfire S127, Reflections S116. Range *$$$ [bar, restaurant, accommodations]*

OTSEGO COUNTY

GAYLORD COUNTRY CLUB (18)
M-32 West, Gaylord. (616) 546-3376.
Looks from road are deceiving; it's good challenging course as it gets back in woods. One of most reasonable prices in north for good golf.
Par 72, 6477 yards. S119. Range *$$ [bar, grill]*

GREEN TREES GOLF (9)
262 N. Townline Rd., 2 miles west of Gaylord off M-32. Gaylord. (517) 732-6006.
Par 29, 1410 yards says it all. Range *$*

HIDDEN VALLEY RESORT & CLUB (18)
696 E. M-32, Gaylord. (517) 732-5181.
One of state's oldest and most comfortable resorts and prototype for many of today's golf and ski operations. Cart required.
Par 71, 6305 yards. S117. Range $$$ *[bar, grill]*

MICHAYWE HILLS GOLF CLUB (36)
1535 Opal Lake Rd., south of city off Old US-27, Gaylord. (517) 939-8911.
Pines Course, par 72, 6900 yards, delightful course and host of 1991 Michigan Amateur Championship. Lake Course, par 72, 6500 yards, designed by Jerry Matthews and voted one of best new resort courses by *Golf Digest* in 1989. Starts through pretty stand of white birch and has some of everything. Cart required.
Lake S131, Pines S124. Range $$$ *[bar, grill]*

TREETOPS - SYLVAN RESORT (18)
3962 Wilkinson Rd., Gaylord. (517) 732-6711 or (800) 444-6711.
Designed by Robert Trent Jones. Signature hole is par 3 sixth where Jones named the course, looking out at miles and miles of treetops. It's tough and it isn't a fast-play course. Owner Harry Melling of Jackson has another course growing in several miles north of the Jones course. It's by hot designer Tom Fazio and it will be challenging but not penal. Golf director Rick Smith is one of state's top teachers and runs weekend and 7-day schools on spacious range. Cart required.
Par 71, 7046 yards. S127. Range $$$$ *[bar, grill, restaurant]*

WILDERNESS VALLEY GOLF CLUB (18)
7519 Mancelona Rd., southwest of Gaylord. (616) 585-7090.
Very enjoyable. A 1979 design by Jerry Matthews. Championship tees stuck back in tunnels but middle and forward tees comfortable. Owner Dave Smith in process of adding second course designed by Tom Doak.
Par 71, 6519 yards. S121. $$ *[bar, grill]*

PRESQUE ISLE COUNTY

ROGERS CITY COUNTRY CLUB (9)
4325 Golf Course Rd., Rogers City. (517) 734-4909.
In process of adding nine holes.
Par 35, 3071 yards. S110. Range *$*

ROSCOMMON COUNTY

BURNING OAK GOLF CLUB (18)
4345 Redwood Dr., Higgins Lake. (517) 821-9821.
Par 72, 6188 yards. S115. Range *$ [bar, grill]*

De CARLO'S BIRCH POINTE GOLF CLUB (9)
7071 Artesia Beach Rd., St. Helen. (517) 389-7009.
Par 36, 3160 yards. *$ [bar, grill]*

PINE VIEW GOLF COURSE (9)
4825 W. Houghton Lake Dr., on M-55 & Townline Rd., Houghton Lake. (517) 366-9806.
Par 36, 3120 yards. *$*

WHITE DEER COUNTRY CLUB (18)
1309 Bright Angel Dr., off M-55, Prudenville. (517) 366-5812.
Par 72, 6400 yards. *$$ [bar, snacks]*

YE OLDE COUNTRY CLUB (9)
904 W. Sunset, Roscommon. (517) 275-5582.
Par 35, 3000 yards. *$ [snacks]*

$ — Greens fee to $15
$$ — Greens fee to $25
$$$ — Greens fee to $50
$$$$ — Greens fee more than $50
Range — Driving range available
S — Slope rating

NORTHWEST MICHIGAN

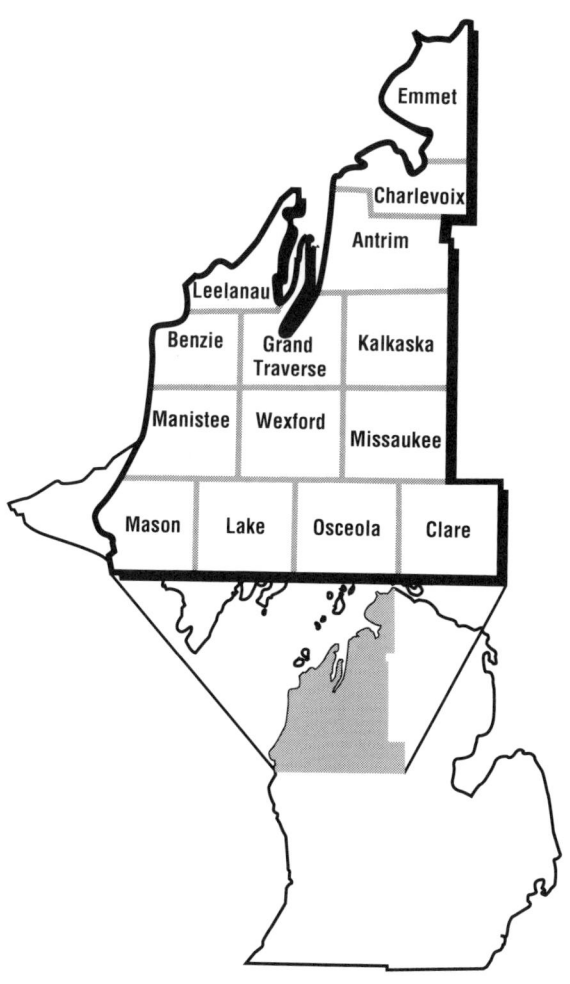

ANTRIM COUNTY

A-GA-MING GOLF CLUB (18)
McLachlan Rd., east of US-31, Elk Rapids. (616) 264-5081.
Overlooks Torch Lake and second nine, added several years ago with design input from PGA Hall-of-Famer Chick Harbert, affords many nice lake views. Harbert summers at A-Ga-Ming, a comfortable course at par 72, 6572 yards. Carts required. S118. Range *$$ [bar, grill]*

ANTRIM DELLS GOLF COURSE (18)
US-31, Atwood. (616) 599-2679.
Highway signs on each end of town proclaim it "Atwood the Adorable" in a jibe at nearby Charlevoix which calls itself "Charlevoix the Beautiful." Jerry Matthews designed Antrim Dells which used to host a Michigan Amateur qualifying round each year when the Amateur was played in Charlevoix. With many OB's, the Dells was not a favorite of the Amateur field.
Par 72, 6600 yards. S121. Range *$$ [bar, restaurant]*

ELK RAPIDS GOLF CLUB (9)
724 Ames, off US-31, Elk Rapids. (616) 264-8891.
For the locals and non-expense accounters. Good food at nearby Elk Rapids Inn. Semi-private on Wednesdays only due to leagues.
Par 36, 2966 yards. S111. *$*

BEL-AIRE GOLF CLUB (9)
M-88, Bellaire. (616) 533-8942.
One par 5 and the rest are 4s with three of them under 300 yards. Little old pine-lined cut-rate course among the $50-$100 tracks. Nice restaurant, the Hearthstone.
Par 37, 3000 yards. Range *$ [bar & grill]*

LAKES OF THE NORTH GOLF COURSE (18)
541 Sky Trails Ct., bet. US-131 & Old 27, Mancelona. (616) 585-6800.
Enjoyable, won't feel exhausted when you finish. Bill Newcomb did second nine which opened in 1989.
Par 72, 6922 yards. S124. Range *$$ [bar, grill]*

SHANTY CREEK RESORT (36)
M-88, Bellaire. (616) 533-8621.
The Legend was designed by Arnold Palmer and partner Ed Seay and it's maturing beautifully. The creek's in play on the 497-yard, par 5 seventh and 351-yard, par 4 eighth, cutting in front of the green on each of these excellent holes. Goofy par 4 second hole (short uphill par 4 with two ravines) is result of Department of Natural Resources strictures. Deskin Course, named for Shanty Creek founder and designed by William Diddel, who did Barton Hills, Bloomfield Hills and Forest Lake in the Detroit area and Hidden Valley in Gaylord, is pretty much wide open. Several new holes are going in so that resort can put in new range.
Legend: par 72, 6764 yards; Deskin: par 71, 6360 yards. Legend S123, Deskin S117. Range $$$$

SCHUSS MOUNTAIN GOLF CLUB (18)
M-88, Mancelona. (616) 587-9232.
Warner Bowen, a Ferris and MSU graduate and one of the state's lesser-known designers, lets his work speak for itself and Schuss is one of the most enjoyable courses in the north; no tricks, no gimmicks and friendly spot owned by former Chicago Bear Vic Zucco with former Golf Professional-of-the-Year Rodger Jabara in the shop. Schuss hosts Michigan PGA's ITT Classic each summer.
Par 72, 7100 yards. S120. Range $$$ *[bar, grill]*

WINDMILL FARMS RESTAURANT & GOLF COURSE (9)
County Rd. 38, 1-1/2 miles east of 131, Mancelona. (616) 587-5258.
Rustic.
Par 27, 795 yards. $

BENZIE COUNTY

CRYSTAL LAKE GOLF CLUB (18)
8493 Fairway Dr., Beulah. (616) 882-4061.
A Matthews father-son collaboration in 1970. Orchardland and nice views of Crystal Lake.
Par 72, 6500 yards. S116. $$ *[bar, grill]*

CRYSTAL MOUNTAIN RESORT (18)
M-115, Thompsonville. (616) 378-2911.
Very popular for price and playability; not as difficult as the big name courses. Bill Newcomb designed second 18 but its first nine not scheduled to open until spring 1992.
Par 72, 6400 yards. S110. Range $$$ [bar, grill]

FRANKFORT GOLF CLUB (9)
2 miles north on M-22, Frankfort. (616) 352-4101.
Par 34, 2500 yards. S107. $ [snacks]

CHARLEVOIX COUNTY

BEAVER ISLAND (9)
Take ferry from Charlevoix. (616) 448-2301.
Island breezes.
Par 35, 3200 yards. $

BELVEDERE GOLF CLUB (18)
Charlevoix. (616) 547-2611.
Private club which permits outside play. One of the very best courses in Michigan and longtime home of Michigan Amateur. Veterans were upset when Amateur moved because Belvedere's practice and clubhouse facilities were inadequate. But just a superb match play course. Old style, small greens puts accent on short game. Tom Watson loved it when he summered in Michigan as kid and it's one of Michigan Hall-of-Famer Chuck Kocsis' favorites.
Par 72, 6715 yards. S122. Range $$$

BOYNE MOUNTAIN RESORT (36)
Deer Lake Rd., Boyne Falls. (616) 549-2441.
Alpine and Monument courses both start from top of backside of Boyne's ski hill. Terrific first tee views after 1-1/2 mile ride up cart path through woods. Bill Newcomb did the Alpine in the 70s and it's one of my favorite northern courses — I aced the third hole. Alpine has a nice flow to it. Monument has a couple of odd doglegs and one of longest bunkers on earth. The island 18th green is not among my favorites. It's more expensive of the two. Also a nine hole short course.
Both are par 72 and have multiple tees of 7,000 yards. Alpine S118. Monument S126. Range $$$ & $$$$ [bar, grill]

CHARLEVOIX GOLF COURSE (9)
400 Central Ave., just off US-31, Charlevoix. (616) 547-3268.
Typical flat resortland municipal nine-holer and nice pocketbook break.
Par 36, 3000 yards. $

DUNMAGLAS GOLF CLUB (18)
Boyne City Rd. bet. Charlevoix & Boyne City. (616) 547-2834.
Scheduled to open in mid-summer 1991. Designed by Larry Mancour, long one of state's best pros and now Senior PGA Tour player, and owner Chuck MacGillivray of Flint. Views of Lakes Charlevoix and Michigan. Hills, valleys, six holes through woods.
Par 72, 6800 yards. Range $$$ *(tentative) [bar, restaurant]*

SPRINGBROOK HILLS GOLF CLUB (18)
Springvale Rd., Walloon Lake. (616) 535-2413.
Price is right.
Par 72, 6200 yards. $ *[bar, grill, restaurant]*

YE NYNE OLDE HOLLES GOLF CLUB (9)
Ironton Ferry Rd., Charlevoix. (616) 582-7609.
Quaint. It's a sidehiller with an I-don't-believe-it ninth green. Nice view of Lake Charlevoix. Friendly place.
Par 35, 2970 yards. $ *[snacks, beer & wine]*

CLARE COUNTY

COUNTY CLARE GOLF CLUB (9)
7795 S. Clare Ave., Clare. (517) 386-3510.
Par 36, 2900 yards. $

THE TAMARACKS GOLF COURSE (9)
8900 N. Clare Ave., Harrison. (517) 539-5441.
Jerry Hawkins and his family built it, own it, work it and plan on adding a second nine.
Par 35, 2900 yards. $

EMMET COUNTY

BOYNE HIGHLANDS RESORT (54)
Hendrick Rd., Harbor Springs. (616) 526-2171.
Three courses, the new Donald Ross Memorial, the original Heather by Robert Trent Jones and the Moor by Bill Newcomb. Boyne founder Everett Kircher hired Jones to do the Heather in 1965 and it's the granddaddy of the northern Michigan golf boom. It also is one of Jones' best works, a big, strong course through wetlands, pines and hardwood. It's especially beautiful during fall color season. It long was ranked among America's Best 100 Golf Courses by *Golf Digest*. The Moor has a lot of water and a zig-zag par 5 18th. The new Ross Memorial is a collection of 17 holes from the old Scottish master's courses including Pinehurst No. 2 and Oakland Hills and it is outstanding and will only get better as it matures. Bowing to Ross's roots, the 14th hole from Royal Dornoch in Scotland, where Ross learned the game, is the 10th hole of the Ross Memorial. The Ross is complemented by a new clubhouse and practice facilities.
Heather: par 72, 7218 yards; Moor: par 72, 7179 yards; Ross: par 72, 6840 yards. Heather S119, Moor S122, Ross S126. Range *$$$ & $$$$* *[bar, grill, two restaurants]*

LITTLE TRAVERSE BAY GOLF CLUB (18)
Clayton Rd., Harbor Springs. (616) 526-9661.
Going to be a run on adjectives when it opens in 1991. First nine scheduled for July 1 and rest by August 1. Twelve holes have views of Little Traverse Bay and designer Jeff Gorney says your jaw will drop on first tee which has a 120-foot drop and lake view. Owner Ed Frey and veteran northern Michigan amateur Phil Harrison had plenty of input.
Par 72, 6850 yards. Range *$$$$*

PINE HILL GOLF CLUB (18)
US-31, Brutus. (616) 529-6574.
Short course, 4600 yards, easy on the wallet.
Narrows: par 35, 3000 yards; Executive: par 29, 1600 yards. Range *$* *[bar, grill]*

WILDERNESS GOLF COURSE (9)
Cecil Bay Rd., Carp Lake. (616) 537-4973.
Hard by Wilderness State Park. Another blue light special.
Par 35, 2600 yards. Range $

GRAND TRAVERSE COUNTY

CEDAR HILLS GOLF COURSE (9)
7525 Cedar Run Rd., Traverse City. (616) 947-8237.
Par 3, 1300 yards. $ *[bar, hot dogs]*

ELMBROOK GOLF COURSE (18)
420 Hammond Rd., Traverse City. (616) 946-9180.
Basic, busy, affordable and hilly. Lot of local play.
Par 72, 6000 yards. S112. $ *[bar, grill]*

GRAND TRAVERSE RESORT GOLF COURSE (36)
US-31, north of M-72, Acme. (616) 938-1620.
The Jack Nicklaus-designed Bear is the most notorious course in the state. Very penal, Michigan Open contestants have shot in the 90s and some have failed to break 100. Small, severely sloped greens, deep bunkers and plenty of water make the Bear live up to its reputation. The Bear has matured nicely since it opened and hosted its first Michigan Open in 1984. With greens fees heading for $100 for walk-ins, it's Michigan's most expensive course. You get superb maintenance for your money and be ready to contribute some golf balls. The Resort Course, renovated by Bill Newcomb, is no slouch. The Open was played there for several years before the Bear was ready and it gave Michigan's best all they wanted and then some.
Both are par 72 and the Bear stretches to 7065 yards. Bear S138, Resort 117. Range *$$$ & $$$$ [bar, grill, several restaurants]*

GREEN HILLS GOLF COURSE (9)
2411 W. Silver Lake Rd., Traverse City. (616) 946-2975.
Wear your hard hat. Very hilly. Price is right.
Par 36, 3400 yards. $ *[bar, grill]*

HIGH POINTE GOLF CLUB (18)
M-72, Williamsburg. (616) 267-9900.
Going into third season and one of more talked-about northern courses. Front nine is open Scottish style; back nine dramatic elevation change and "Up North" characteristics — white pine, hardwood, ups and downs. Designer Tom Doak used fescue grass for fairways and greens instead of bent. Fescue requires less water, chemicals and fertilizer. Also permits more severe undulations on greens because it is slower than bent. Blind dogleg 10th and wetlands zig-zagged 18th cause problems.
Par 71, 6819 yards. S122. Range *$$$ [bar, grill]*

INTERLOCHEN GOLF CLUB (18)
US-31, Interlochen. (616) 275-7311.
Half flat, half hilly, piney, well-maintained, nice restaurant and with National Music Academy close by, should be able to make those clubs sing.
Par 71, 6040 yards. Range *$$ [bar, grill, restaurant]*

MITCHELL CREEK COUNTRY CLUB (9)
2846 Three Mile Rd., Traverse City. (616) 941-5200.
Busy spot for the locals and low budget vacationers.
Par 36, 3200 yards. Range *$ [bar, grill]*

KALKASKA COUNTY

TWIN BIRCH GOLF COURSE (18)
County Road, 1 mile east of M-72 and US-131 intersection, Kalkaska. (616) 258-9691.
Recently added second nine. Nice affordable course through pines with water, creek or pond, in play on nine holes. No. 1 handicap hole is 381-yard second which will catch water with long drive.
Par 5s are short: 468, 462, 417 and 476. Par 72, 6133 yards. S113. Range *$$ [bar, grill]*

LAKE COUNTY

MARQUETTE TRAILS GOLF COURSE (18)
Rt. 1, Big Star Lake Rd., Baldwin. (616) 898-2450.
Sleeper and only track in the county.
Par 70, 5600 yards. Range *$$ [bar, grill]*

LEELANAU COUNTY

DUNES GOLF CLUB (9)
M-72, 3 miles south of Glen Lake, 17 miles west of Traverse City, Empire. (616) 326-5390.
Nice little par 36, 3200 yards in one of state's beauty spots. *$ [snacks]*

MATHESON GREENS GOLF CLUB (9)
Thomas Rd., CR 633, 4 miles southwest of Northport. (616) 386-5122.
Par 72, 6645 yards. Range *$$*

SUGAR LOAF RESORT (18)
4500 Sugar Loaf Mountain Rd., Cedar. (616) 228-5461.
Jan Stephenson's name is on the course and while she's a summer visitor, it was there before she got there. One nine is through cherry orchards and other nine is rolling. More bunkers and water on first nine — only seven bunkers on second nine.
Par 72, 6800 yards. S118. Range *$$$ [bar, grill, restaurant, children's programs]*

VERONICA VALLEY GOLF COURSE (9)
Lake Leelanau Dr. (CR 641), 5 miles south of Lake Leelanau, Lake Leelanau. (616) 256-9449.
Scheduled to open spring 1991.
Par 35, 3203 yards. *$*

MANISTEE COUNTY

BEAR LAKE GOLF ASSOCIATION (18)
S-31, 1 mile south of Bear Lake. (616) 864-3817.
Par 72, 6000 yards. *$$*

FAWN CREST GOLF COURSE (9)
663 Seaman Rd., Wellston. (616) 848-4174.
Par 31, 2000 yards. *$*

FOX HILLS GOLF COURSE (9)
485 Fox Farm Rd., 4 miles south of Manistee. (616) 723-3809.
Par 33, 2050 yards. *$*

MANISTEE GOLF & COUNTRY CLUB (18)
500 Cherry Rd., Manistee. (616) 723-2509.
Par 70, 6000 yards and views to Lake Michigan. A Bruce Matthews design.
S115. Range *$$ [bar, grill]*

MASON COUNTY

LAKESIDE LINKS GOLF COURSE (18)
5369 W. Chauves Rd., Ludington. (616) 843-3660.
Nice, playable, lake breezes and catches downstaters on their way up US 31, the "scenic route" north.
Par 70, 6000 yards. Range *$$ [bar, grill, restaurant]*

MISSAUKEE COUNTY

MISSAUKEE GOLF COURSE (18)
5300 S. Morey, M-66 and M-55, Lake City. (616) 825-2756.
Got the only game in the county and the course is well-conditioned.
Par 71, 6061 yards. *$*

OSCEOLA COUNTY

SPRING VALLEY (18)
7637 W. US-10, Hershey. (616) 832-5041.
What golf boom? Hard to imagine a whole county and only one course.
Par 72, 6300 yards. Range *$ [bar, grill]*

WEXFORD COUNTY

BRIAR VALLEY GOLF COURSE (9)
5441 E. M-115, Mesick. (616) 885-1220.
Narrow, through woods.
Par 34, 2550 yards. Range *$*

CADILLAC COUNTRY CLUB (18)
M-55, Cadillac. (616) 775-9442.
Old style, round greens, good condition and pro Dave Kendall will give you lesson with the long putter. Carts mandatory.
Par 70, 6000 yards. S117. Range *$$$ [bar & grill for members only]*

LAKEWOOD ON THE GREEN GOLF COURSE (9)
128 Lakewood Dr., Cadillac. (616) 775-4763.
Well-maintained, woodsy.
Par 35, 2900 yards. *$ [sandwiches]*

MCGUIRE'S GOLF RESORT (27)
7880 Mackinaw Trail, Cadillac. (616) 775-9949.
Bruce Matthews designed it. 18-hole course is par 71, 6524 yards, 9-holer is par 36, 2792 yards. Popular resort, lot of pines, good maintenance and views of Lake Mitchell.
Range *$$$ [bar, grill]*

$ — Greens fee to $15
$$ — Greens fee to $25
$$$ — Greens fee to $50
$$$$ — Greens fee more than $50
Range — Driving range available
S — Slope rating

UPPER PENINSULA

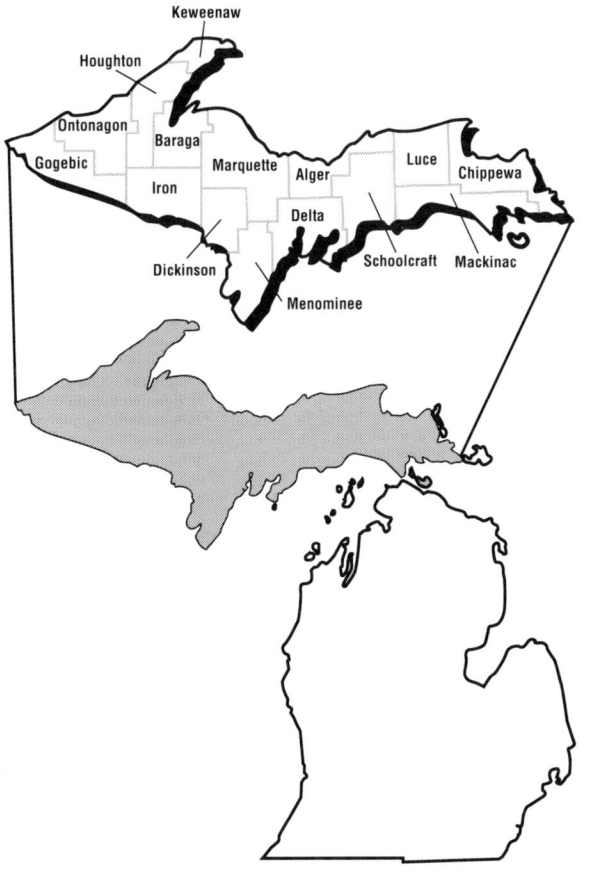

ALGER COUNTY

PICTURED ROCKS GOLF & COUNTRY CLUB (9)
on H-58, 3 miles east of Munising. (906) 387-2146.
Nice nine-holer in Michigan's waterfall county, one of the prettiest counties in the state.
Par 36, 3210 yards. Range *$ [bar, grill]*

BARAGA COUNTY

L'ANSE GOLF CLUB (9)
Golf Course Rd., L'Anse. (906) 524-6600.
Flat, wide open.
Par 36, 3265 yards. *$ [bar, grill]*

CHIPPEWA COUNTY

DRUMMOND ISLAND GOLF COURSE (9)
Next to the airport, Drummond Island. (906) 493-5406.
Tourists fly in to play The Rock, Tigers boss Tom Monaghan's well-groomed layout, but the islanders play this nine-holer and it's a busy if unspectacular one.
Par 36, 3128 yards. Range *$*

KINCHELOE MEMORIAL PUBLIC GOLF COURSE (18)
Exit 378 off I-75, east to Kinross. (906) 495-5706.
Rated in *GOLF* magazine's "50 Best Bangs for a Buck" in 1989. Par 72, 7100 yards on former Kincheloe Air Force Base and signature hole is a 140-yard, par 3 over an immense bunker. Call for tee time. S124. Range *$$ [bar, grill]*

MUNOSCONG GOLF CLUB (9)
M-129, Pickford. (906) 647-9812.
At the eastern edge of the U.P.
Par 36, 3250 yards. *$ [snacks]*

THE ROCK GOLF COURSE (18)
Domino's Lodge, Drummond Island. (906) 493-1000.
Pizza magnate Tom Monaghan's retreat is about 90 minutes east of the Mackinac Bridge and off the southeast corner of the U.P. Designer Harry Bowers' first solo effort after working for Robert Trent Jones is a beauty and while challenging, it isn't Jones-tough. Lots of wildlife including bear. Course literally blasted out of the limestone that forms the island.
Par 71, 6830 yards. S134. Range *$$$$ [bar, grill]*

SAULT STE. MARIE COUNTRY CLUB (18)
1520 Riverside Dr., Sault Ste. Marie. (906) 632-7812.
It's where Gordie Howe and the Red Wings played when the club trained in the Soo years ago. Bossman Jack Adams thought walking was good for the legs and the players didn't object.
Par 71, 6350 yards. Range *$$*

DELTA COUNTY

COUNTRY MEADOWS GOLF COURSE (9)
4688 12th Rd., Escanaba. (906) 786-1565.
Par 36, 3100 yards. *$*

ESCANABA COUNTRY CLUB (18)
1800 11th Ave. S., Escanaba. (906) 786-4430.
Second nine opens this year, lot of water on it.
Par 71, 6500 yards. *$ [bar, grill]*

GLADSTONE GOLF CLUB (18)
6514 Days River, Gladstone. (906) 428-9646.
Hilly, tree-lined, little stream, good spot.
Par 72, 6500 yards. Range *$ [bar, grill]*

HIGHLAND GOLF CLUB (18)
US-2 and US-41, 7 miles west of Escanaba. (906) 466-7457.
Relatively flat and short, small greens, good condition. Call for tee time.
Par 71, 6442 yards. *$ [bar, grill]*

NAHMA (9)
LL Rd., Nahma. (906) 644-2648.
Par 36, 2800 yards. $

TERRACE BLUFF COUNTRY CLUB (18)
7527 Lake Bluff 19.4 Rd., Gladstone. (906) 428-2343.
Overlooks north shore of Lake Michigan, lot of views, lot of pines. Good course.
Par 69, 6168 yards. Range $$ [bar, grill]

DICKINSON COUNTY

OAK CREST GOLF COURSE (18)
on Hwy. US-8, Norway. (906) 563-5891.
Nice city-owned pine and oak-lined course with new irrigation system.
Par 72, 6100 yards. S112. Range $ [bar, grill]

PINE GROVE COUNTRY CLUB (18)
1520 W. Hughitt, Iron Mountain. (906) 774-3493.
Old, traditional course has reputation as perhaps best course in the U.P., "like a second Augusta National." Chicagoan Lawrence Packard did second nine — he also did Leslie Park in Ann Arbor and Hampshire in Dowagiac which are fine courses. Call for tee time. Men only Sat-Sun mornings.
Par 72, 6660 yards. S123. Range $$$ [bar, grill]

PINE MOUNTAIN GOLF COURSE (9)
Pine Mountain Lodge, Iron Mountain. (906) 774-2747.
Too bad they don't put a tee on top of the giant Pine Mountain Ski Jump — they'd have the most spectacular first tee in the state.
Par 34, 2527 yards. $ [bar]

GOGEBIC COUNTY

GOGEBIC COUNTRY CLUB (9)
Country Club Rd., south of US-2, Ironwood. (906) 932-2515.
Par 35, 3000 yards. $ [bar, grill]

Jack Berry's Guide to Michigan Golf

INDIANHEAD MOUNTAIN RESORT (9)
500 Indianhead Rd., off US-2, 1 mile west of Wakefield. (906) 229-5181.
Located at U.P.'s busiest ski resort. Skiing's obviously No. 1.
Par 27, 980 yards. $ *[bar, grill]*

HOUGHTON COUNTY

CALUMET GOLF CLUB (9)
Golf Course Rd., off US-41, Calumet. (906) 337-3911.
Some fine views of Lake Superior.
Par 36, 3150 yards. Range $ *[bar, grill]*

PORTAGE LAKE GOLF COURSE (18)
Michigan Tech University, Houghton. (906) 487-2641.
University's course. Older nine short and flat, newer nine by Jerry Matthews more exciting.
Par 72, 6300 yards. S114. Range $

WYANDOTTE HILLS GOLF CLUB (9)
M-26 next to Twin Lakes State Park, west of Toivola. (906) 288-3720.
Par 34, 2665 yards. $ *[bar, grill]*

IRON COUNTY

CRYSTAL FALLS GOLF COURSE (9)
On Wagner St., next to the river, Crystal Falls. (906) 875-9919.
Par 36, 3000 yards. $

GEORGE YOUNG'S GOLF COURSE (18)
Hwy. 424, Young's Lane, Gaastra. (906) 265-3401.
Young built it himself and took 15-20 years to do it. Young died in the mid-1980s but course is financed through an endowment. Long, pretty views and challenging.
Par 72, 7100 yards. $

IRON RIVER COUNTRY CLUB (9)
Seldon Rd., Iron River. (906) 265-3161.
Mining company built it for its executives many years ago and then taken over by locals.
Par 36, 3300 yards. Range $ *[bar, grill]*

KEEWEENAW COUNTY

KEEWEENAW MT. LODGE (9)
US-41, Copper Harbor. (906) 289-4403.
As far north as you can go and play golf in Michigan. Rustic nine-holer of 3189 yards and par 36 where there's never a wait at the first tee. Built during the Depression with an eye to drawing tourists up to play golf. Plans called for 18 but money ran out and now there's talk of adding the second nine.
$ [bar, grill]

LUCE COUNTY

NEWBERRY COUNTRY CLUB (9)
at M-123 & M-28, Newberry. (906) 293-8422.
Sporty, well-kept.
Par 35, 2900 yards. Range *$ [bar, grill]*

MACKINAC COUNTY

GRAND HOTEL (9)
Mackinac Island. (906) 847-3331.
They call this nine-holer, renovated for the 1987 season by Jerry Matthews, "The Jewel." It would be difficult to pick a prettier setting in the state and it's worth packing your clubs on the trip for fudge. Twin it with Wawashkamo Golf Club for a different and memorable experience. Lunch at the Grand Stand, another special touch. Open May 10 to October 30.
Par 33, 2700 yards. S104. *$$ [bar, grill, restaurant]*

HIAWATHA SPORTSMEN'S CLUB (9)
Engadine. (906) 477-6683.
A very short summertime course. *$*

LES CHENEAUX (9)
Snows Channel, Cedarville. (906) 484-3606.
Par 35, 3000 yards. *$*

ST. IGNACE (9)
US-2, 1 mile west of St. Ignace. (906) 643-8071.
Great views of the Straits and the Mackinac Bridge. Nice little course.
Par 36, 3100 yards. *$*

WAWASHKAMO GOLF CLUB (9)
Mackinac Island. (906) 847-3871.
Claims to be oldest continuously played nine-hole course in Michigan. Scottish pro Alex Smith laid it out in 1898 on upper part of island where British and Americans fought in 1814. It's a National landmark and Michigan Historic Site. It's 3019 yards, par 36 with a charm of its own — don't expect Oakland Hills conditions.
S111. $ *[snacks]*

MARQUETTE COUNTY

MARQUETTE GOLF & COUNTRY CLUB (18)
Grove St., Marquette. (906) 225-0721.
Lot of hills, trees, bunkers (75) and play — 35,000 to 40,000 rounds despite one of state's shortest seasons. Semi-private club has 700 members and 100 on the waiting list so if you want to play, arrange in advance. Must call for tee time.
Par 71, 6200 yards. S114. Range $$ *[bar, grill]*

K.I. SAWYER GOLF COURSE (18)
K.I. Sawyer AFB, Gwinn. (906) 346-2026.
New nine is shorter than old nine but is tight and challenging.
Par 70, 6136 yards. Range $ *[grill]*

WAWONOWIN COUNTRY CLUB (18)
County Rd. 478, Ishpeming. (906) 485-1435.
Original nine was typical — short and small greens. New nine (about 15 years old) added excitement. One of U.P.'s best.
Par 72, 6300 yards. Range $$ *[bar, grill]*

MENOMINEE COUNTY

NORTH SHORE GOLF CLUB (18)
Hwy. M-35, 6 miles north of Menominee. (906) 863-8421.
Newer nine (the front) more challenging.
Par 72, 6500 yards. $$ *[bar, grill]*

ONTONAGON COUNTY

BIG SPRUCE GOLF COURSE (9)
US-45, north of Bruce Crossing. (906) 827-3727.
Short but fun.
Par 35, 2600 yards. *$ [bar, grill]*

ONTONAGON GOLF CLUB (9)
North of M-28, 1 mile east of Ontonagon. (906) 884-4130.
Another of state's many shorties.
Par 35, 2700 yards. *$ [bar, snacks]*

SCHOOLCRAFT COUNTY

INDIAN LAKE GOLF & COUNTRY CLUB (9)
3 miles north of Manistique. (906) 341-2330.
Excellent greens and it's right on Indian Lake. Call for tee time.
Par 36, 3100 yards. *$ [bar, grill]*

THE SCOOP ON SLOPE

Slope is the United States Golf Association's course rating system and formula which makes it possible to equalize play for traveling golfers. For courses that have been sloped, this Guide contains the middle marker rating, which may be different than the slope rating in other listings. The average USGA slope rating for both men and women is 113.

Slope takes into account topography of fairways and greens, rough, severity of bunkers, water hazards, green speed and the psychological effect of all of these as well as yardage. I feel it is a more accurate degree of course difficulty for the average player than the course rating.

Course rating numbers are fine for scratch players but the USGA says the average player has a 20 handicap.

Take Salem Hills in Washtenaw County and the Lakes Course at Michaywe Hills in Otsego County. From the middle markers, Salem's course rating is 70.7. Michaywe Lakes is 71.0. you can't get much closer. But for the 20-handicapper, Michaywe Lakes is a much more difficult course because of its many hazards which produce double bogeys and worse. Consequently, Michaywe Lakes' slope rating is 131 while Salem Hills is 116 so make your first tee games accordingly.

Two hundred and fifteen Michigan public courses have been slope-rated by the Golf Association of Michigan since the program began in 1983 under Joe Luyckx. Counting private courses, the GAM has rated 355 courses and is just about halfway through the task of sloping all Michigan courses.

The USGA wants all courses sloped but courses which do not belong to the Association don't have to do it. Public courses that have been sloped tell the public they care, so a slope rating is a little like a Michelin or Mobil star.

The GAM has 35 trained men and women volunteer raters who work season-long in teams of three or four.

DESIGNS ON GOLF

As the Sundance Kid said to Butch Cassidy, "Who ARE those guys?!"

Indeed, who ARE those guys who have marched inexorably across Michigan designing new golf courses?

Jack Nicklaus, Arnold Palmer and Robert Trent Jones have gotten the most notoriety for the Bear, the Legend, the Heather and Treetops, all northern resort courses, but more golf is played on courses by Bruce and Jerry Matthews, Jeff Gorney, Bill Newcomb, Mark De Vries, Warner Bowen and Art Hills. Most of them learned their trade at Michigan State and most have stayed in Michigan to design courses.

Jerry Matthews of Lansing is the busiest in-state designer followed by Bill Newcomb of Ann Arbor. Mark De Vries of Grand Rapids is No. 3 in volume of in-state work closely followed by Jeff Gorney of Grand Rapids with Warner Bowen of Sheridan and Harry Bowers of Novi trailing them.

Art Hills of Sylvania, Ohio, is one of the leading national designers but he still has kept his green thumb in a number of significant state projects.

Easterner Tom Doak liked Michigan so much that he decided to move to Traverse City after designing High Pointe.

Old-time designers Donald Ross, Wilfrid Reid, William Connellan and William Diddle contributed more than 50 years ago.

Probably the biggest change in golf course design is the move to the air game. Beginning with the Old Course at St. Andrews, the game was played on the ground — bump and run the ball onto the green. After World War II, designers began to force the player to fly the ball to the green. They put water in front of the green or deep bunkers.

New look penal golf has resulted in five- and six-hour rounds and it has increased golf ball sales because so many splash into those ponds.

Bruce Matthews was Michigan's most prolific

designer and his trademark was playable courses. Translation: not penal. Born in 1904, Matthews graduated from Michigan State in 1925 with a bachelor's degree in landscape architecture. His first design was Manistee Country Club in 1929. When the Depression hit, he became manager and superintendent at Green Ridge Country Club in Grand Rapids. He held that job until 1959, designing courses on the side.

Bruce Matthews was joined by his son, Jerry, also an MSU alumnus, in 1959 and the firm designed more than 75 new courses and remodeled more than 150. Amazingly, the Matthews have worked on more than one-quarter of Michigan's courses.

Bruce retired to Grand Haven Country Club, which he designed and owns, and Jerry took over the firm. Jerry's nephew, Bruce, also is with the firm, the third generation Matthews.

Jerry Matthews started in the footsteps of his father but now makes his own way, designing more radically with a greater use of hazards. Matthews said golfers have become accustomed to the tougher courses on their excursions to resorts such as Myrtle Beach and will pay more to play the courses that are designed tougher and require more maintenance.

Matthews' newest works are Elk Ridge at Atlanta, the Lakes Course at Michaywe Hills in Gaylord and Timber Ridge in East Lansing. All are dramatic and challenging.

Indiana-born Bill Newcomb is a 1963 University of Michigan architecture graduate who went on to take a master's degree in landscape architecture. Newcomb won the Indiana Open as an amateur and won the 1967 Michigan Amateur. He apprenticed to Pete Dye from 1965-67 before going on his own.

Newcomb's best-known Michigan works are the Alpine Course at Boyne Mountain, the Moor at Boyne Highlands, the Resort Course at Grand Traverse Resort and Willow Metropark in suburban Detroit. Newcomb has remodeled many private clubs around Detroit including Plum Hollow and Barton Hills in Ann Arbor.

Mark De Vries is a 1949 MSU graduate who worked for the Grand Rapids Parks and Recreation Department in landscape architecture before striking out on his own in golf course design in 1963. Chase Hammond in Muskegon and Saskatoon perhaps are his best west Michigan works and on the east side he did two of Livonia's fine courses, Whispering Willows and Fox Creek plus Springfield Oaks, most challenging of the Oakland County Recreation Department's four courses.

Jeff Gorney is a native of Jackson with a bachelor's degree in landscape architecture from MSU plus a degree in turfgrass management.

"I felt if I was going to design golf courses, I should learn how to maintain them," Gorney said of his return to MSU for the turfgrass degree. Then he spent 11 years as superintendent of the Elks Club at Grand Rapids before moving full-time into design.

"I see a lot of beautiful stuff by some designers but I think of the maintenance headaches they cause so I avoid that. I'm basically in the service business — I design what the owner wants and I work with him." Gorney designed nine new holes for Mike Hill's Heart of the Lakes course in Brooklyn, the new Fox Run in Grayling and two more projects will open this year, both with fine lake views, Little Traverse Bay Club in Harbor Springs and Lakeview Hills in Lexington.

Warner Bowen of Sheridan is that rarity among golf course designers — he shies away from publicity. Bowen's top project now is a complete renovation of busy Dearborn Hills from a somewhat nondescript, 18-hole, 5600-yard course into a challenging executive course.

Bowen, a graduate of Ferris State and Michigan State, did Schuss Mountain's popular course as well as Rogue River in Sparta and Benona Shores in Muskegon.

Harry Bowers, another MSU alumnus, worked for Robert Trent Jones during the design and construction of Treetops at Sylvan Resort. He went on his own with The Rock at Domino's Lodge on Drummond Island. That was a real challenge: Drummond is the third largest freshwater island in the world and it is a solid hunk of limestone. Dynamiters from the island's quarries blasted trenches for the irrigation lines and topsoil and sand had to be barged up to the island at the head of Lake Huron.

Bowers came up with a design that accents Drummond Island's rugged beauty.

Ohioan Art Hills has a lot of Michigan in him. He has a bachelor's degree from MSU and master's from Michigan and he worked on the greens crew at Barton Hills while attending Michigan. Hills is one of the country's busiest and best designers, in demand by private clubs, resorts and the public sector. He's designed 11 Michigan courses and remodeled or renovated twice that number.

Hills' new 36-hole Egypt Valley Country Club opens outside Grand Rapids in 1991 while he continues to draw praise from the three public courses he designed around Detroit, Pine Trace in Rochester Hills, Golden Fox in Plymouth and Taylor Meadows in Taylor. His second nine of the Honors Course at Oak Pointe in Brighton is progressing and he re-did the tees and bunkers on Oakland Hills' championship South Course in preparation for the 1991 U.S. Senior Open.

Tom Doak traveled to Scotland, Australia and New Zealand to get a feel for the old masters and that's particularly evident on the front nine of High Pointe near Traverse City. Doak now is working on a second course at Wilderness Valley between Mancelona and Gaylord.

Jet-setters who've left their mark in Michigan are Robert Trent Jones, who started the designer trend and northern Michigan golf boom at Boyne Highlands in 1965. It long ranked as one of America's best 100 courses. Jones returned several years ago to do Treetops at Sylvan Resort.

Jack Nicklaus designed the Bear at Grand Traverse and they don't come any tougher — tiny greens, deep bunkers, decked fairways, wetlands, ponds and a creek; it is a masochist's delight and precisely what developer Paul Nine ordered.

Arnold Palmer and partner Ed Seay did the Legend at Shanty Creek and after some early problems with greens, it's maturing into a handsome course.

Tom Fazio is the latest design superstar to land in Michigan. His works include nationally-acclaimed Wild Dunes, Butler National, Pinehurst No. 6, Black Diamond and Lake Nona.

Fazio started with his uncle, the late George Fazio who was one of golf's top players in the 1940s and 50s. George lost the 1950 U.S. Open playoff to Ben Hogan. Tom joined his uncle in 1962 and by the late 1970s was handling the bulk of the work.

The Fazio course at Treetops may open this fall but certainly in 1992. It's in a series of valleys and has only one water hole, most unusual for a new course and most welcome for the average resort course player.

PUBLIC COURSES by DESIGNER

Here is a list of some of the better-known designers and the Michigan public courses that they have had a hand in developing.

Warner Bowen
Alpena Golf Club
Benona Shores Golf Course
Centennial Acres Golf Course
Holland Lake Golf Course
Schuss Mountain Golf club

Harry Bowers
The Rock Golf Course

Harry Bowers & Frank Godwin
Marion Oaks

George Catto
Hickory Hill Golf Club

Donald Chilkis and Robert Bills
Gaylord Country Club
Green Oaks Golf Course
Maple Leaf Golf Course
Marysville Golf Course
Michaywe Hills Golf Club, Pine Course
Red Oaks Golf Course
Stony Creek Metropark
Wawonowin Country Club

William Connellan and Wilfrid Reid
Bald Mountain Golf Course
Brae Burn Golf Course

William Diddel
Deskin Course at Shanty Creek Resort
Hidden Valley Resort

Mark De Vries
Alpine Golf Club
Brayside, The Golf Club at Courtland Hills
Chase Hammond Golf Course
Fox Creek Golf Course
Saskatoon Golf Club

Springfield Oaks
Tyler Creek Golf Course
Western Greens Country Club
Whispering Willows

Tom Doak
High Pointe Golf Club

Ernie Fuller
Links at Pinewood Golf Club

Jeff Gorney
Fox Run Country Club
Grayling Country Club
Hill's Heart of The Lakes
Little Traverse Bay Golf Club

Walter Hagen, Bill Newcomb & Jeff Gorney
Lakeview Hills Golf Course

Chick Harbert
A-Ga-Ming Golf Club

Robert Bruce Harris
Heather Highlands Golf Club

Jerry Hawkins
The Tamaracks Golf Course

Art Hills
Fox Hills Country Club
Giant Oak Golf Club
Honors Course at Oak Pointe Golf Club
Pine Trace Golf Club
Taylor Meadows Golf Club

Robert Trent Jones
Heather at Boyne Highlands
Treetops at Sylvan Resort

Karl Litten
Huron Golf Club

Chuck MacGillivray & Larry Mancour
Dunmaglas Golf Club

Larry Mancour
Grand Blanc Country Club

Jack Matthias and Gene LaFramboise
Thunder Bay Golf Course

Bruce Matthews
Blossom Trails Golf Course
Forest Akers Golf Course
Grand Haven Golf Club
Independence Green Executive Golf Course
Manistee Golf & Country Club
McGuire's Golf Resort (with Mark De Vries)
Southmoor Golf Course
Tyrone Hills
White Birch Hills Golf Course

Jerry Matthews
Antrim Dells Golf Course
Bird Creek Golf Club
Candlestone Inn & Golf Resort
Cracklewood Golf Club
Elk Ridge Golf Course
Grand Hotel
Lakewood Shores Resort
Links of Novi
Michaywe Hills Golf Club, Lakes Course
Portage Lake Golf Course
San Marino Golf Course
Shenandoah Country Club
Sugar Springs Country Club
Sycamore Hills Golf Club
Timber Ridge Golf Course
Wilderness Valley Golf Club
Wolverine Golf Club & Banquet Center

Bruce Matthews & Jerry Matthews
Crystal Lake Golf Club
Lake O' The Hills Golf Course
Lincoln Hills Golf Course
Salem Hills Golf Club
Terra Verde Golf Club

Robert Bruce Harris & Bruce Matthews
Old Channel Trail Golf Course

Don McKinley
Pine Valley Golf Club

Grant McKinley
Brigadoon Golf Club

Desmond Muirhead
Bay Valley Golf Club

Bill Newcomb
Moor at Boyne Highlands
Alpine at Boyne Mountain
Crystal Mountain Resort
Resort Course at Grand Traverse Resort Golf Course
Huron Breeze Golf & Country Club
Lakes of The North Golf Course
Pebble Creek Golf Club
Riverview Highlands Golf Course
Willow Metropark Golf Course

Jack Nicklaus
The Bear at Grand Traverse Resort Golf Course

Ron Otto
Garland Resort

Lawrence Packard
Hampshire Country Club
Pine Grove Country Club

Arnold Palmer & Ed Seay
The Legend at Shanty Creek Resort

Lou Powers
Rattle Run Golf Course

Donald Ross
Rogell GC
Rackham Golf Course
Warren Valley Golf Course

Charlie Scott
  Binder Park Golf Course
  Lake Doster Golf Club
  Stonehedge Golf Course

Alex Smith
  Wawashkamo Golf Club

Al Watrous
  Mission Hills Golf Club

George Young
  George Young's Golf Course

WHY DID THEY NAME IT?

There's usually a good explanation, but it isn't always obvious. Here are the stories behind some of the most interesting and unusual course names.

CRACKLEWOOD: When the Penzien brothers, developers of the Macomb County course with their uncle, Joa Penzien, started hitting practice shots during construction, they found a lot of the shots hit trees and, well, crackled.

CROCKERY HILLS: It's in Crockery Township and near Crockery Creek in Ottawa County, north of I-96 between Grand Rapids and Muskegon. The Ottawa tribe settled the area and found the clay made good crockery and over the years, it keeps popping up.

DUNMAGLAS: Chuck MacGillivray of Flint is the developer of this new course on the north side of Lake Charlevoix and he named it after the ancestral home of the MacGillivray Clan in Scotland.

GARLAND: Founder Herman Otto named his northern getaway lodge and nine hole course at Lewiston after his manufacturing company in Detroit.

HIDDEN VALLEY: The property of northern Michigan's oldest ski resort-golf course looks dead flat from M-32 just a few blocks east of downtown Gaylord. But drive in to the main lodge and take a peek out the back windows. It's a major league WOW! A deep valley and trees as far as the eye can see.

OT-WELL-EGAN: A play on its location near Ottawa, Plainwell and Allegan.

STONEHEDGE: When designer Charlie Scott, son of Gull Lake View and Bedford Valley owner Darl Scott, walked the land of the family's new property east of Kalamazoo, he was struck by all the stone fences built by farmers who had cleared the land. They were stone hedges.

TREETOPS: Designer Robert Trent Jones picked the name when he stood at the top of the hill looking out over the valley at Sylvan Resort that stretches miles into the distance. "All you can see are treetops," Jones said. Then he added "Treetops is tops."

WAWASHKAMO: Chippewa Chief Eagle Eye (honest) watched some golfers flail away on a course built on the old British-American 1814 battleground on Mackinac Island. The course was built by Scottish professional Alex Smith in 1898. The chief said the golfers "wa-wash-kamo." Translation: They walked a crooked path. Obviously they couldn't hit it straight then, either. Wawashkamo is a National Landmark and a Michigan Historic Site.

WHIFFLETREE HILLS: There really isn't a whiffle tree, like a maple or an elm. The course was built on a dairy farm and a whiffletree — a piece of wood — is part of the equipment to harness horses side-by-side.

HOT DOGS WITH A VIEW

After a long round of golf, nothing beats a snack and a refreshing beverage—all the better if you can see the action while you relax.

Michaywe Lakes Course. If only they could erase that water tower in the distance.

Treetops 11th hole. Sustenance needed after playing 10 and 11, two of the toughest holes on the course.

Elk Ridge. Forget the tube steak, the word here is Honey Baked Ham.

Boyne Heather. Watch them drown those Titleists and Top-Flites in the 18th-hole lake.

Grand Traverse Resort, the Resort Course upper deck. Good view of two water-fronted greens. Listen to those groans.

The Deck at **Country Club of Boyne,** overlooking the 18th green of the Ross Course. Watch the splashes on one of the toughest par 4s in the state.

Schuss Mountain. Wetlands and wet goods.

BEST VIEWS

In addition to great golf, many Michigan courses offer spectacular views. Here are some of my favorites.

BEST FIRST TEES

Boyne Alpine: A mile and a half cart ride up through the woods and then a lovely view of tranquil Deer Lake.

Boyne Monument: Same ride and a downhill par 5 to start with.

BEST SIXTH TEE
Treetops: Par 3 with a 100-foot drop and out there are millions and millions (or is it billions?) of trees.

BEST 10TH TEES
Elk Ridge: Similar to Treetops' sixth although green is framed by striking stand of white birch.

Michaywe Lakes: King of the Hill. Too bad they can't get rid of the distant smokestack.

TREES

Joyce Kilmer would have had a field day, wooden you know, with Michigan's treed golf courses.

We've got Beech Woods, Birchwood, Briarwood, Cherrywood, Red Cedar, Hickory Hill, Maple Lane, Sycamore Hill and Whispering Willows.

But more oaks and pines have taken root in Michigan public golf course names than any of their leafy cousins.

Oak is No. 1. Twenty-three courses have the sturdy tree in their names including an Oakland Hills in Calhoun County and another in Kalamazoo County. There are Twin Oaks in Clinton and Saginaw counties. In Berrien County it's simply The Oaks.

Giant Oak says it all in Monroe County. The specimen oak near the first green and second tee of the Temperance course is said to be 300 years old and has a diameter of more than 10 feet.

Pines are the close runner-up in the tree contest — 21 courses have pine in their name including a trio of Pineviews in Roscommon, St. Joseph and Washtenaw counties and a pair of The Pines, one in Isabella County, the other in Kent.

GOLF SCHOOLS

Nick Faldo does it. So does Jack Nicklaus. And so does practically every professional on every tour. They all take lessons. David Leadbetter completely restructured Faldo's game and converted him from a representative player to a champion.

Nicklaus worked with the late Jack Grout for four decades. On the eve of the Golden Bear's Senior Tour debut in The Tradition last year at Desert Highlands in Scottsdale, Arizona, Nicklaus spotted PGA Teacher of the Year Jim Flick in his gallery during a practice round.

Because he'd been spending more time on his course design ventures than in competition and on his game, Nicklaus was playing terribly and had lost his confidence. He asked Flick for help and they went right to the practice tee where Flick worked with him over two days. Nicklaus blew away the field.

That's the value of instruction. If a champion can be helped, imagine what lessons will do for hackers and intermediate golfers and nothing beats intensive instruction.

Five Michigan resorts offer comprehensive golf schools: Boyne USA, Crystal Mountain, Garland, Grand Traverse Resort and Treetops.

Boyne offers a "Super Five" package which is a five day combination of daily lessons, golf on its five courses plus lodging, breakfast and dinner for $750. The sessions begin June 9 and continue for 10 weeks.

Crystal Mountain presents Rick Davenport's Academy Golf. The 1990 five-day, four-night rate was $490 and the two-night, three day weekend was $360. That included all meals.

Garland professional Lee Woodruff, the 1990 Michigan PGA Match Play champion, will operate a school July 1-4 and it will include all meals, lodging and golf for $1200.

The nationally-known John Jacobs Practical Golf School operates throughout the summer at Grand Traverse Resort. The five-day, four night double occupancy rate this year is $895 ($1090 single) and the weekend rate is $495 double ($595 single).

Treetops' Rick Smith is an excellent young instructor who fits instruction to the pupil. Smith isn't a one-method man. Three rising PGA Tour stars — Rocco Mediate, Billy Andrade and Lee Janzen — are among his students and biggest boosters.

And, on a personal note, Smith turned my wife into a semi-golf nut, so much so that on one cold, windy, wet late September morning in northern Michigan, she said "What a great day to play golf!" Honest. We played 36 that day.

Smith's longtime friend, Henry Young, is co-director of the Treetops school and you can sign up for three-day midweek or weekend sessions. Prices last year were $972 per person double occupancy for the three day, three night mid-week school and $668 double occupancy for the weekend two day/two night school.

By the numbers:

BOYNE: (800) 632-7174
CRYSTAL MOUNTAIN: (800) 321-4637
GARLAND: (800) 678-4952
GRAND TRAVERSE RESORT:
   (800) 748-0303
TREETOPS: (800) 444-6711

TOURNAMENT COURSES

How does your game stack up against, say Chi Chi Rodriguez? Or Michigan Open champions Randy Erskine, Fred Muller and Buddy Whitten? Or Michigan Amateur champion Pete Green?

Baseball fans don't get the opportunity to try for the short porch in Tiger Stadium's right field and football fans don't run punts back in Spartan Stadium or the Silverdome. Basketball fans don't go one-on-one with Isiah Thomas in The Palace.

But golfers do get the chance to play in some of the game's great arenas, from the Old Course at St. Andrews, Scotland, to, say, Belvedere Golf Club in Charlevoix, former longtime home of the Michigan Amateur and just a classic old course with small greens that call for accurate approaches or delicate chips. PGA Tour star Dan Pohl won two Michigan Amateurs at Belvedere and Tom Watson, who spent his boyhood summers at nearby Walloon Lake, counted Belvedere among his favorite courses.

Among the tournament courses open to public play in Michigan are the Bear and Resort courses at Grand Traverse Resort. Chi Chi Rodriguez won the Senior PGA Tour's Ameritech Senior Open on the Jack Nicklaus-designed Bear last summer. The Bear is the home of the Michigan Open and before that it was the Resort course, also a demanding test.

Bedford Valley in Battle Creek was the Michigan Open's home from 1970-77 and then hosted the Michigan Public Links Championship for several years and it's a good, strong, no-nonsense golf course.

Michaywe's Pines course hosts the Michigan Amateur in 1991 and Boyne's courses have hosted the Michigan State Pro-Amateur Championship and the Great Lakes Senior Golf Association's annual championship.

Salem Hills in suburban Detroit has been qualifying course for the PGA Tour's Buick Open for several years and in southwest Michigan, Hampshire and Lake Michigan Hills serve as qualifying sites for the prestigious Western Amateur which draws the cream of America's amateur talent, players on their way to the PGA Tour.

Gull Lake View entertained the Michigan Seniors Publinx Golf Association Championship and the Pines in Weidman hosted eight Michigan Public Links Championships.

Bay Valley was opened by Jack Nicklaus and the Bay County course also has hosted the Michigan Women's Amateur Championship as has Verona Hills in the Thumb.

Championship golf is all around us in Michigan.

TRIPS

You don't have to go to Myrtle Beach to get a golf package. Many Michigan regions offer golf packages. Numbers where you can get information include:

Boyne Country Convention & Visitors Bureau: (800) 845-2828

Discover Golf on the Sunrise Side: (800) SAY-YES3

East Lansing Comfort Inn: (517) 349-8700

Gaylord/Otsego County Convention & Tourism Bureau: (800) 345-8621

Grand Traverse Convention & Visitors Bureau: (800) 872-8377

Kalamazoo County Convention & Visitors Bureau: (616) 381-4003

Northwest Michigan Golf Council: (800) 937-7272

PAR Golf (northern Michigan resorts): (800) 222-2220

Radisson Resort & Conference Center (Ypsilanti): (800) 333-3333

Stouffer Battle Creek Hotel: (616) 963-7050

SHOPS

As one might expect, Michigan also has a wealth of golf shops throughout the state. A partial list of some of the more prominent ones follows.

Southwest

BOBICK'S GOLFLAND, 6396 Gull Rd. (M 43), Kalamazoo. (616) 342-0381

GOLF SERVICES INC., 6958 W. Main St., 1 mile west of US 131, Kalamazoo. (616) 372-5956

KALAMAZOO GOLF CENTER, 8536 Shaver Rd., Kalamazoo. (616) 323-0757.

West

GOLF FACTORY, 4028 West River Dr., N.E., Comstock Park. (616) 784-3459.

GOLFHAUS, 1541 28th St., S.W., Wyoming. (616) 531-1990.

THE GOLF CENTER, 2280 Broomfield Road, Mt. Pleasant. (517) 772-0156.

THE GOLF PLACE, 1781 5th St., Muskegon. (616) 725-9450.

GOLF USA, 5747 28th St., S.E., Cascade. (616) 531-3531.

PIONEER GOLF, 3242 Leonard, N.W., Walker. (616) 791-9611.

PRO GOLF DISTRIBUTORS, 644 28th St., S.W., Wyoming. (616) 531-7780.

SCOTT'S GOLF CENTER, 3227 28th St., N.W., Grandville. (616) 538-7651.

TEE 2 GREEN, 5300 Northland Dr., N.E., Grand Rapids. (616) 363-1111.

Central

BEECHWOOD GREENS, 1161 W. Frances, Mt. Morris. (313) 686-4200.

THE CLUB HOUSE, 5048 Page Avenue, Jackson. (517) 764-5127.

COLEMAN GOLF CENTER, 3573 Shaffer Rd., Coleman. (517) 465-6052.

GOLF HAUS, 700 N. Pennsylvania at Saginaw, Lansing. (517) 482-8842.

GOLF SERVICES INC., 2828 E. Grand River, Lansing. (517) 372-2260.

GOLF USA, 1420 E. Michigan, Lansing. (517) 372-1611.

KEN'S HOLE-IN-ONE GOLF SHOP INC., 3191 Smithville, Eaton Rapids. (517) 663-1191.

KING PAR, Flushing Rd. & Linden, Flushing. (313) 732-2470.

LANSING GOLF CENTER, 5855 M 99, Dimondale. (517) 646-8555.

MC SPORTING GOODS, 5002 W. Saginaw, Lansing. (517) 323-1663.

MC SPORTING GOODS, Meridian Mall, Okemos. (517) 349-3700.

PRO GOLF DISCOUNT, 5441 W. Saginaw, Lansing. (517) 321-7568.

PRO GOLF DISCOUNT, 1869 West Grand River, Okemos. (517) 349-8750.

SEIFERT GOLF PLUS, 2193 Grand Blanc Rd., 1/4 mile east of US 23, Grand Blanc. (313) 655-8070.

Detroit & Southeast Michigan

A-1 GOLF HOSPITAL, 1517 N. Main, Royal Oak. (313) 545-3711.

BAVARIAN VILLAGE SKI & GOLF, Woodward & Square Lake Rd., Bloomfield Hills. (313) 338-0803.

BAVARIAN VILLAGE SKI & GOLF, Novi Town Center, South of Twelve Oaks Mall, Novi. (313) 347-3322.

BOB MOSS'S BETTER GOLF CENTER, 2502 Woodward, Bloomfield Hills. (313) 335-4653.

BRIGHTON GOLF CENTER, 8509 Grand River, Brighton. (313) 227-4404.

BUTASH-PROFESSIONAL GOLF CLUB REPAIR, 925 S. Main, Royal Oak. (313) 545-6968.

CADDYSHACK, 2137 W. Stadium Blvd., Ann Arbor. (313) 662-7744.

CADDYSHACK, 114 W. Grand River, Brighton. (313) 227-3388.

CADDYSHACK, 21750 Hall Rd. (M 59), Clinton Township. (313) 463-9334.

CADDYSHACK, 36750 Garfield, Clinton Township. (313) 979-1360.

CADDYSHACK, 31205 Orchard Lake Rd., Farmington Hills. (313) 626-2185.

CADDYSHACK, 371010 6 Mile Rd., Livonia. (313) 464-6581.

CADDYSHACK, 32501 Van Dyke, Warren. (313) 979-1360.

CARL'S GOLFLAND, 1976 S. Telegraph Rd., Bloomfield hills. (313) 335-7762.

CLASSIC CUSTOM GOLF CLUBS & REPAIR, 36356 Ford Road, Westland. (313) 729-9450.

DEWULF GOLF CLUB REPAIR CENTER, 304 S. Telegraph, Pontiac. (313) 681-8948.

FALCON GOLF, 24000 N. Woodward, Pleasant Ridge. (313) 547-4800.

GOLF SHOP, 38180 Utica, Sterling Heights. (313) 978-8778.

GORMAN GOLF PRODUCTS INC., 24250 12 Mile Rd., at Telegraph, Southfield. (313) 549-0050.

GREEN OAKS GOLF COURSE PRO SHOP, 1775 Clark Road, East Ypsilanti. (313) 485-0881.

HICKORY WOODS GOLF COURSE PRO SHOP, 5415 Craine, Pittsfield Township. (313) 434-4653.

JAWOR'S GRATIOT GOLF, 32900 Gratiot at 14 Mile Rd., Roseville. (313) 293-9836.

JAWOR'S USA SPORTS, 141 S. Opdyke, 1/4 mile south of the Silverdome, Auburn Hills. (313) 332-2268.

JP GOLF, 875 Wing, Plymouth. (313) 455-4653.

KAREN PEEK'S GOLF PRO SHOP, 10100 W. 10 Mile, Huntington Woods. (313) 398-8430.

LAS VEGAS DISCOUNT GOLF & TENNIS, 42663 Ford Rd., Canton Township. (313) 981-4900.

Shops

NEVADA BOB'S, 2903 Carpenter, Ann Arbor. (313) 973-1500.

NEVADA BOB'S, 23902 Ford Rd., Dearborn Heights. (313) 274-4701.

NEVADA BOB'S, 33220 West 12 Mile Rd., Farmington Hills. (313) 471-4477.

NEVADA BOB'S, 3793 Rochester Rd. at M 59, Rochester. (313) 852-6110.

NEVADA BOB'S, 14439 Eureka, Southgate. (313) 284-6880.

NEVADA BOB'S, 40742 Van Dyke at 18 Mile, Sterling Heights. (313) 268-4550.

NEVADA BOB'S, 7084 Highland Rd., Atlas Plaza, Waterford. (313) 666-4242.

PALMER PARK GOLF SHOP, 199013 Woodward, Detroit. (313) 883-5343.

PRO GOLF DISTRIBUTORS, 4949 Washtenaw, Ann Arbor. (313) 434-4300.

PRO GOLF DISTRIBUTORS, 37320 7 Mile Rd., Livonia. (313) 464-0882.

PRO GOLF DISTRIBUTORS, 24909 Plymouth Rd., Redford. (313) 532-2800.

PRO GOLF DISTRIBUTORS, 1914 S. Rochester Rd., Rochester. (313) 656-9110.

PRO GOLF DISTRIBUTORS, 30150 Gratiot, Roseville. (313) 778-0200.

PRO GOLF DISTRIBUTORS, 610 N. Woodward, Royal Oak. (313) 542-4973.

PRO GOLF DISTRIBUTORS, 13248 Fort St., Southgate. (313) 285-7820.

PRO GOLF DISTRIBUTORS, 13963 Hall Rd., Mt. Clemens. (313) 247-4300.

PRO GOLF DISTRIBUTORS, 2530 Orchard Lake Rd., Sylvan Lake. (313) 681-7780.

RICK'S GOLF INC., 2645 W. Houghton Lake Drive, Prudenville. 517-366-6458.

R&R GOLF, 540 Highland Ave, Milford. (313) 685-2928.

SOUTHLAND GOLF CENTER INC., 11125 Reeck, Southgate. (313) 374-2211.

THREE PUTT PRO SHOP, 39500 Five Mile, Norvl Twp. (313) 420-2228.

TRAVIS POINTE GOLF COURSE PRO SHOP, 2829 Travis Pointe Road, Ann Arbor. (313) 662-0946.

WESTBROOK GOLF COURSE PRO SHOP, 17666 Grand River, Novi. (313) 349-2723.

Northeast

ALPENA GOLF COURSE PRO SHOP, 6373 Werth Road, Alpena. (517) 354-4312.

DENNIS DUFINA GOLF SHOP, 6373 Werth Rd., NW Chisholm-Downtown Alpena. (517) 354-4312.

Northwest

BOYNE COUNTRY SPORTS, Boyne Highlands Resort, Harbor Springs. (616) 526-2171.

EAGLE GOLF OUTFITTERS, 3100 W. Houghton Lk. Dr., Houghton Lake. (517) 366-6616.

FORE SEASONS GOLF, 926 South Airport Rd., Traverse City. (616) 947-0666.

Shops

GRAND TRAVERSE RESORT GOLF CENTER, 4263 East M-72, Acme. (616) 938-5416.

GREAT NORTH SPORTS, Downtown Traverse City. (616) 946-3290.

JOE'S GOLF WORKS, 405 N. Divisions Rd., Petoskey. (616) 347-7203.

MAIN STREAM SPORTS, 222 N. Mitchell St., Cadillac. (616) 775-8700.

MAINSTREAM SPORTS, 1251 N. South Airport, Traverse City. (616) 946-1181.

NORTHWIND SPORTS, US 31 N. near M-55, Manistee. (616) 723-2255.

PRO GOLF DISCOUNT, 1235 East Front, Traverse City. (616) 941-2224.

PRO SPORTS CENTER, Schuss Mountain, Mancelona. (616) 587-5355. THE SPORTS PEDDLER, 441 E. Mitchell, Petoskey. (616) 347-5580.

Upper Peninsula

BUSTER'S SPORTS SHOP, 123 Cleveland Avenue, Ishpeming. (906) 486-8800.

ESCANABA COUNTRY CLUB GOLF SHOP, Escanaba. (906) 786-4430.

GLADSTONE COUNTRY CLUB GOLF SHOP, Days River, Gladstone. (906) 428-9646.

GOGEBIC COUNTRY CLUB GOLF SHOP, Country Club Road, Ironwood. (906) 932-2515.

HIGHLAND PRO SHOP, off US 2 and 41, Escanaba. (906) 466-7457.

MARQUETTE GOLF AND COUNTRY CLUB PRO SHOP, Grove Street, Marquette. (906) 225-0721.

SAULT ST. MARIE GOLF COURSE PRO SHOP, Sault Country Club, Sault St. Marie. (906) 632-7812.

TERRACE BLUFF, 7527 Lake Bluff, Gladstone. (906) 428-2343.

WAWONOWWIN PRO SHOP, 3432 Country Road 478, Champion. (906) 485-1435.

Michigan Counties and their respective regions in this Guide.

Alcona	Northeast
Alger	Upper Peninsula
Allegan	Southwest
Alpena	Northeast
Antrim	Northwest
Arenac	Northeast
Baraga	Upper Peninsula
Barry	Southwest
Bay	Mid-Mich., East
Benzie	Northwest
Berrien	Southwest
Branch	Southwest
Calhoun	Southwest
Cass	Southwest
Charlevoix	Northwest
Cheboygan	Northeast
Chippewa	Upper Peninsula
Clare	Northwest
Clinton	Mid-Mich., West
Crawford	Northeast
Delta	Upper Peninsula
Dickinson	Upper Peninsula
Eaton	Southwest
Emmet	Northwest
Genessee	Mid-Mich., East
Gladwin	Northeast
Gogebic	Upper Peninsula
Grand Traverse	Northwest
Gratiot	Mid-Mich., West
Hillsdale	South Central
Houghton	Upper Peninsula
Huron	Mid-Mich., East
Ingham	South Central
Ionia	Mid-Mich., West
Iosco	Northeast
Iron	Upper Peninsula
Isabella	Mid-Mich., West
Jackson	South Central
Kalamazoo	Southwest
Kalkaska	Northwest
Keweenaw	Upper Peninsula
Kent	Mid-Mich., West
Lake	Northwest
Lapeer	Mid-Mich., East
Leelanau	Northwest
Lenawee	South Central
Livingston	Wash-Liv-Monroe
Luce	Upper Peninsula
Macomb	Macomb-St. Clair
Mackinac	Upper Peninsula
Manistee	Northwest

Marquette	Upper Peninsula
Mason	Northwest
Mecosta	Mid-Mich., West
Menominee	Upper Peninsula
Midland	Mid-Mich., East
Missaukee	Northwest
Monroe	Wash-Liv-Monroe
Montcalm	Mid-Mich., West
Montmorency	Northeast
Muskegon	Mid-Mich., West
Newaau	Mid-Mich., West
Oakland	Oakland
Oceana	Mid-Mich., West
Ogemaw	Northeast
Ontonagon	Upper Peninsula
Osceola	Northwest
Oscoda	Northeast
Otsego	Northeast
Ottawa	Mid-Mich., West
Presque Isle	Northeast
Roscommon	Northeast
Saginaw	Mid-Mich., East
Sanilac	Mid-Mich., East
Schoolcraft	Upper Peninsula
Shiawassee	Mid-Mich., East
St. Clair	Macomb-St. Clair
St. Joseph	Southwest
Tuscola	Mid-Mich., East
Van Buren	Southwest
Washtenaw	Wash-Liv-Monroe
Wayne	Wayne
Wexford	Northwest

ALPHABETICAL LIST OF MICHIGAN'S PUBLIC GOLF COURSES

The county and the corresponding region in this Guide (unless the county is treated as a region) are noted in parentheses.

Wayne   3
Oakland   11
WLM: Washtenaw, Livingston, & Monroe   29
SCen: South Central   37
SW: Southwest   45
MME: Middle Michigan East   57
MMW: Middle Michigan West   67
MSC: Macomb & St. Clair   21
NE: Northeast   81
NW: Northwest   91
UP: Upper Peninsula   103

A-GA-MING GOLF CLUB, Elk Rapids (Antrim, NW)
ALPENA GOLF CLUB, Alpena (Alpena, NE)
ALPINE GOLF CLUB, Comstock Park (Kent, MMW)
ALWYN DOWNS, Marshall (Calhoun, SW)
ANTRIM DELLS GOLF COURSE, Atwood (Antrim, NW)
ARCADIA HILLS GOLF COURSE, Attica (Lapeer, MME)
ARROWHEAD GOLF CLUB, Auburn Hills (Oakland)
ARROWHEAD GOLF COURSE, Lowell (Kent, MMW)
ARROWHEAD GOLF & COUNTRY CLUB, Caro (Tuscola, MME)
BALD MOUNTAIN GOLF COURSE, Lake Orion (Oakland)
BAY COUNTY GOLF COURSE, Essexville (Bay, MME)
BAY VALLEY GOLF CLUB, Bay City (Bay, MME)
BEAR LAKE GOLF ASSOCIATION, Bear Lake (Manistee, NW)
BEAVER ISLAND, Beaver Island (Charlevoix, NW)
BEDFORD VALLEY GOLF COURSE, Battle Creek (Calhoun, SW)
BEECH HOLLOW GOLF COURSE, Freeland (Saginaw, MME)
BEECH WOODS GOLF CENTER, Southfield (Oakland)
BEECHWOOD GREENS GOLF COURSE, Mt Morris (Genesee, MME)
BEL-AIRE GOLF CLUB, Bellaire (Antrim, NW)
BELLE ISLE GOLF COURSE, Detroit (Wayne)
BELLE RIVER GOLF & COUNTRY CLUB, Memphis (St Clair, MSC)
BELLO WOODS GOLF COURSE, Mt Clemens (Macomb, MSC)
BELVEDERE GOLF CLUB, Charlevoix (Charlevoix, NW)

BENONA SHORES GOLF COURSE, Shelby (Oceana, MMW)
BENT PINE GOLF CLUB, Whitehall (Muskegon, MMW)
BIG SPRUCE GOLF COURSE, Bruce Crossing (Ontonagon, UP)
BINDER PARK GOLF COURSE, Battle Creek (Calhoun, SW)
BIRCHWOOD GOLF COURSE, Howard City (Montcalm, MMW)
BIRD CREEK GOLF CLUB, Port Austin (Huron, MME)
BLOSSOM TRAILS GOLF COURSE, Benton Harbor (Berrien, SW)
BOGIE LAKE GOLF CLUB, Union Lake (Oakland)
BONNIE BROOK GOLF COURSE, Detroit (Wayne)
BONNIE VIEW GOLF COURSE, Eaton Rapids (Eaton, SW)
BOYNE HIGHLANDS RESORT, Harbor Springs (Emmet, NW)
BOYNE MOUNTAIN RESORT, Boyne Falls (Charlevoix, NW)
BRAD VAN PELT'S GOLF COURSE, Owosso (Shiawasse, MME)
BRAE BURN GOLF COURSE, Plymouth (Washtenaw, WLM)
BRAMBLEWOOD GOLF COURSE, Holly (Oakland)
BRANSON BAY GOLF COURSE, Mason (Ingham, SCen)
BRAYSIDE, THE GOLF CLUB AT COURTLAND HILLS, Rockford (Kent, MMW)
BRIAR HILL GOLF COURSE, Fremont (Newaygo, MMW)
BRIAR VALLEY GOLF COURSE, Mesick (Wexford, NW)
BRIARWOOD GOLF CLUB, Caledonia (Kent, MMW)
BRIGADOON GOLF CLUB, Grant (Newaygo, MMW)
BROADMOOR COUNTRY CLUB, Caledonia (Kent, MMW)
BRONSON GOLF COURSE, Bronson (Branch, SW)
BROOKLANE GOLF COURSE, Northville (Wayne)
BROOKSHIRE INN & GOLF COURSE, Williamston (Ingham, SCen)
BROOKSIDE GOLF COURSE, Gowen (Montcalm, MMW)
BROOKSIDE GOLF COURSE, Saline (Washtenaw, WLM)
BROOKWOOD GOLF COURSE, Buchanan (Berrien, SW)
BRUCE HILLS GOLF CLUB, Romeo (Macomb, MSC)
BRYN MAWR GOLF CLUB, Dowagiac (Cass, SW)
BURNING OAK GOLF CLUB, Higgins Lake (Roscommon, NE)
BURR OAK GOLF COURSE, Parma (Jackson, SCen)
BUTTERNUT BROOK GOLF COURSE, Charlotte (Eaton, SW)

Alphabetical List of Public Courses

BYRON HILLS GOLF COURSE, Byron Center (Kent, MMW)
CADILLAC COUNTRY CLUB, Cadillac (Wexford, NW)
CALUMET GOLF CLUB, Calumet (Houghton, UP)
CANDLESTONE INN & GOLF RESORT, Belding (Ionia, MMW)
CARLETON GLEN GOLF CLUB, Carleton (Monroe, WLM)
CARO GOLF CLUB, Caro (Tuscola, MME)
CASCADES GOLF COURSE, Jackson (Jackson, SCen)
CASEVILLE GOLF COURSE, Caseville (Huron, MME)
CEDAR CREEK GOLF CLUB, Battle Creek (Calhoun, SW)
CEDAR GLEN GOLF CLUB, New Baltimore (Macomb, MSC)
CEDAR HILLS GOLF COURSE, Traverse City (Grand Traverse, NW)
CEDAR VALLEY GOLF CLUB, Comins (Oscoda, NE)
CENTENNIAL ACRES GOLF COURSE, Sunfield (Eaton, SW)
CENTERVIEW, Adrian (Lenawee, SCen)
CENTURY OAKS GOLF COURSE, Elkton (Huron, MME)
CHANDLER PARK GOLF COURSE, Detroit (Wayne)
CHARDELL GOLF COURSE, Bath (Clinton, MMW)
CHARLEVOIX GOLF COURSE, Charlevoix (Charlevoix, NW)
CHASE HAMMOND GOLF COURSE, Muskegon (Muskegon, MMW)
CHEBOYGAN GOLF & COUNTRY CLUB, Cheboygan (Cheboygan, NE)
CHERRYWOOD GOLF CLUB, Ottawa Lake (Monroe, WLM)
CHESHIRE HILLS GOLF COURSE, Allegan (Allegan, SW)
CHIPPEWA HILL COUNTRY CLUB, Durand (Shiawasse, MME)
CHISHOLM HILLS GOLF COURSE, Lansing (Ingham , SCen)
CLARK LAKE GOLF COURSE, Brooklyn (Jackson, SCen)
CLARKSTON GOLF CLUB, Clarkston (Oakland)
CLEARBROOK GOLF CLUB, Saugatuck (Allegan, SW)
CLINTON COUNTY COUNTRY CLUB, St Johns (Clinton, MMW)
CONCORD HILLS GOLF COURSE, Concord (Jackson, SCen)
CORUNNA HILLS GOLF COURSE, Corunna (Shiawasse, MME)
COUNTRY CLUB OF REESE, Reese (Saginaw, MME)
COUNTRY MEADOWS GOLF COURSE, Escanaba (Delta, UP)
COUNTY CLARE GOLF CLUB, Clare (Clare, NW)
CRACKLEWOOD GOLF CLUB, Mt Clemens (Macomb, MSC)

Jack Berry's Guide to Michigan Golf

CRAPO HILLS GOLF COURSE, West Branch (Ogemaw, NE)
CRESTVIEW, Kalamazoo (Kalamazoo, SW)
CRESTVIEW GOLF CLUB, Zeeland (Ottawa, MMW)
CROOKED CREEK GOLF COURSE, Saginaw (Saginaw, MME)
CRYSTAL FALLS GOLF COURSE, Crystal Falls (Iron, UP)
CRYSTAL GOLF COURSE, Crystal (Montcalm, MMW)
CRYSTAL LAKE GOLF CLUB, Beulah (Benzie, NW)
CRYSTAL MOUNTAIN RESORT, Thompsonville (Benzie, NW)
CURRIE GOLF COURSE, Midland (Midland, MME)
DAMA GOLF CLUB, Howell (Livingston, WLM)
De CARLO'S BIRCH POINTE GOLF CLUB, St Helen (Roscommon, NE)
DEARBORN HILLS GOLF COURSE, Dearborn (Wayne)
DEER RUN GOLF CLUB, Lowell (Kent, MMW)
DEER RUN GOLF CLUB, Horton (Jackson, SCen)
DEME ACRES GOLF COURSE, Petersburg (Monroe, WLM)
DeMOR HILLS GOLF COURSE, Morenci (Lenawee, SCen)
DEVIL'S LAKE GOLF COURSE, Manitou Beach (Lenawee, SCen)
DIAMOND LAKE GOLF CLUB, Cassopolis (Cass, SW)
DOWAGIAC ELKS GOLF COURSE, Dowagiac (Cass, SW)
DRUMMOND ISLAND GOLF COURSE, Drummond Island (Chippewa, UP)
DUN ROVIN, Plymouth (Wayne)
DUNDEE GOLF CLUB, Dundee (Monroe, WLM)
DUNES GOLF CLUB, Empire (Leelanau, NW)
DUNHAM HILLS GOLF CLUB, Milford (Oakland)
DUNMAGLAS GOLF CLUB, Boyne City (Charlevoix, NW)
DUTCH HOLLOW GOLF CLUB, Durand (Shiawassee, MME)
EASTERN HILLS GOLF CLUB, Kalamazoo (Kalamazoo, SW)
EDGEWOOD FOREST GOLF COURSE, Prescott (Ogemaw, NE)
EDGEWOOD HILLS COUNTRY CLUB, St Louis (Gratiot , MMW)
EDMORE GOLF COURSE, Edmore (Montcalm, MMW)
EL DORADO COUNTRY CLUB, Mason (Ingham, SCen)
EL DORADO GOLF COURSE, Walled Lake (Oakland)
ELK RAPIDS GOLF CLUB, Elk Rapids (Antrim, NW)
ELK RIDGE GOLF COURSE, Atlanta (Montmorency, NE)
ELLA SHARP PARK GOLF COURSE, Jackson (Jackson, SCen)
ELMBROOK GOLF COURSE, Traverse City (Grand, Traverse NW)
EMS LINKS GOLF COURSE, Sandusky (Sanilac, MME)

Alphabetical List of Courses

ENGLISH HILLS GOLF COURSE, Grand Rapids (Kent, MMW)
ESCANABA COUNTRY CLUB, Escanaba (Delta, UP)
EVERGREEN GOLF COURSE, Hudson (Lenawee, SCen)
EVERGREEN HILLS, Southfield (Oakland)
FAIRVIEW HILLS GOLF CLUB, Mio (Oscoda, NE)
FAIRWAY GOLF CLUB, Hudsonville (Ottawa, MMW)
FAULKWOOD GOLF CLUB, Howell (Livingston, WLM)
FAWN CREST GOLF COURSE, Wellston (Manistee, NW)
FELLOWS CREEK GOLF COURSE, Canton (Wayne)
FERN HILL GOLF & COUNTRY CLUB, Mt Clemens (Macomb, MSC)
FOREST AKERS GOLF COURSE, East Lansing (Ingham, SCen)
FORT GRATIOT GOLF RESORT, Port Huron (St Clair, MSC)
FOUR WINDS GOLF COURSE, East Lansing (Ingham, SCen)
FOX CREEK GOLF COURSE, Livonia (Wayne)
FOX HILLS COUNTRY CLUB, Plymouth (Washtenaw, WLM)
FOX HILLS GOLF COURSE, Manistee (Manistee, NW)
FOX RUN COUNTRY CLUB, Grayling (Crawford, NE)
FRANKENMUTH GOLF CLUB, Frankenmuth (Saginaw, MME)
FRANKFORT GOLF CLUB, Frankfort (Benzie, NW)
FRUITPORT COUNTRY CLUB, Muskegon (Muskegon, MMW)
GARLAND RESORT, Lewiston (Oscoda, NE)
GARVER LAKE GOLF COURSE, Edwardsburg (Cass, SW)
GAUSS' GREEN VALLEY GOLF COURSE, Jackson (Jackson, SCen)
GAYLORD COUNTRY CLUB, Gaylord (Otsego, NE)
GENESEE VALLEY MEADOWS, Swartz Creek (Genesee, MME)
GEORGE YOUNG'S GOLF COURSE, Gaastra (Iron, UP)
GIANT OAK GOLF CLUB, Temperance (Monroe, WLM)
GLADSTONE GOLF CLUB, Gladstone (Delta, UP)
GLADWIN HEIGHTS GOLF COURSE, Gladwin (Gladwin, NE)
GLEN OAKS GOLF COURSE, Farmington Hills (Oakland)
GLENBRIER GOLF COURSE, Perry (Shiawassee, MME)
GLENHURST GOLF COURSE, Redford Township (Wayne)
GLENLORE GOLF COURSE, Milford (Oakland)
GLENN SHORES GOLF CLUB, South Haven (Allegan, SW)
GOGEBIC COUNTRY CLUB, Ironwood (Gogebic, UP)
GOODRICH COUNTRY CLUB, Goodrich (Genesee, MME)
GRACEWIL COUNTRY CLUB, Grand Rapids (Kent, MMW)

Jack Berry's Guide to Michigan Golf

GRACEWIL PINES GOLF COURSE, Jackson (Jackson, SCen)
GRAND BEACH GOLF COURSE, New Buffalo (Berrien, SW)
GRAND BLANC COUNTRY CLUB, Grand Blanc (Genesee, MME)
GRAND HAVEN GOLF CLUB, Grand Haven (Ottawa, MMW)
GRAND HOTEL, Mackinac Island (Mackinac, UP)
GRAND ISLAND GOLF RANCH, Belmont (Kent, MMW)
GRAND LEDGE COUNTRY CLUB, Grand Ledge (Eaton, SW)
GRAND PRAIRIE, Kalamazoo (Kalamazoo, SW)
GRAND RAPIDS GOLF CLUB, Grand Rapids (Kent, MMW)
GRAND TRAVERSE RESORT GOLF COURSE, Acme (Grand Traverse, NW)
GRATIOT COUNTRY CLUB, Ithaca (Gratiot, MMW)
GRAYLING COUNTRY CLUB, Grayling (Crawford, NE)
GREEN ACRES GOLF COURSE, Bridgeport (Saginaw, MME)
GREEN HILLS GOLF COURSE, Pinconning (Bay, MME)
GREEN HILLS GOLF COURSE, Traverse City (Grand Traverse, NW)
GREEN MEADOWS GOLF COURSE, Monroe (Monroe, WLM)
GREEN OAKS, Ypsilanti (Washtenaw, WLM)
GREEN TREES GOLF, Gaylord (Otsego, NE)
GREEN VALLEY GOLF & HEALTH CLUB, Sturgis (St Joseph, SW)
GREENBRIAR, Brooklyn (Jackson, SCen)
GREENBRIER GOLF COURSE, Mayville (Lapeer, MME)
GREENBUSH GOLF COURSE, Greenbush (Alcona, NE)
GROESBECK GOLF COURSE, Lansing (Ingham, SCen)
GULL LAKE VIEW GOLF CLUB, Augusta (Kalamazoo, SW)
GUN RIDGE GOLF COURSE, Hastings (Barry, SW)
HADLEY ACRES GOLF COURSE, Hadley (Lapeer, MME)
HAMPSHIRE COUNTRY CLUB, Dowagiac (Cass, SW)
HAMPTON GOLF CLUB, Rochester Hills (Oakland)
HANKARD HILLS GOLF COURSE, Pleasant Lake (Jackson, SCen)
HARBOUR CLUB GOLF COURSE, Belleville (Wayne)
HARLEY'S GOLF COURSE & RESTAURANT, Union Lake (Oakland)
HARTLAND GLEN GOLF & COUNTRY CLUB, Hartland (Oakland)
HAWTHORNE VALLEY GOLF COURSE, Westland (Wayne)
HEATHER HIGHLANDS GOLF CLUB, Holly (Oakland)
HEATHER HILLS GOLF COURSE, Almont (Macomb, MSC)

Alphabetical List of Courses

HIAWATHA SPORTSMEN'S CLUB, Engadine (Mackinac, UP)
HICKORY HILL GOLF CLUB, Wixom (Oakland)
HICKORY HILLS GOLF COURSE, Jackson (Jackson, SCen)
HICKORY HOLLOW GOLF COURSE, Mt Clemens (Macomb, MSC)
HICKORY KNOLL GOLF COURSE, Whitehall (Muskegon, MMW)
HICKORY WOODS, Ypsilanti (Washtenaw, WLM)
HIDDEN VALLEY GOLF COURSE, Shelbyville (Allegan, SW)
HIDDEN VALLEY RESORT & CLUB, Gaylord (Otsego, NE)
HIGH POINTE GOLF CLUB, Williamsburg (Grand Traverse, NW)
HIGHLAND GOLF CLUB, Escanaba (Delta, UP)
HIGHLAND HILLS GOLF CLUB, DeWitt (Clinton, MMW)
HIGHLAND HILLS GOLF CLUB, Highland (Oakland)
HILL'S HEART OF THE LAKES, Brooklyn (Jackson, SCen)
HILLTOP GOLF COURSE, Plymouth (Wayne)
HOLIDAY GREENS, Mt Pleasant (Isabella, MMW)
HOLLAND COUNTRY CLUB, Holland (Ottawa, MMW)
HOLLAND LAKE GOLF COURSE, Sheridan (Montcalm, MMW)
HUDSON MILLS GOLF COURSE, Dexter (Washtenaw, WLM)
HURON BREEZE GOLF & COUNTRY CLUB, Au Gres (Arenac, NE)
HURON GOLF CLUB, Ypsilanti (Washtenaw, WLM)
HURON HILLS GOLF COURSE, Ann Arbor (Washtenaw, WLM)
HURON MEADOWS GOLF COURSE, Brighton (Livingston, WLM)
HURON SHORES GOLF CLUB, Port Sanilac (Sanilac, MME)
IDYL WYLD, Livonia (Wayne)
INDEPENDENCE GREEN EXECUTIVE GOLF COURSE, Farmington Hills (Oakland)
INDIAN HILLS GOLF COURSE, Okemos (Ingham, SCen)
INDIAN LAKE GOLF & COUNTRY CLUB, Manistique (Schoolcraft, UP)
INDIAN LAKE HILLS GOLF COURSE, Eau Claire (Berrien, SW)
INDIAN RIVER GOLF CLUB, Indian River (Cheboygan, NE)
INDIAN RUN GOLF CLUB, Portage (Kalamazoo, SW)
INDIAN SPRINGS GOLF COURSE, Clarkston (Oakland)
INDIAN TRAILS GOLF COURSE, Grand Rapids (Kent, MMW)
INDIANHEAD MOUNTAIN RESORT, Wakefield (Gogebic, UP)

INTERLOCHEN GOLF CLUB, Interlochen (Benzie, NW)
IRON RIVER COUNTRY CLUB, Iron River (Iron, UP)
IRONWOOD GOLF CLUB, Howell (Livingston, WLM)
IRONWOOD GOLF COURSE, Byron Center (Kent, MMW)
IYOPAWA ISLAND GOLF COURSE, Coldwater (Branch, SW)
JENKINS PUBLIC GOLF COURSE, Litchfield (Hillsdale, SCen)
JEPTHA LAKE GOLF COURSE, Bloomingdale (Van Buren, SW)
KATKE GOLF COURSE, Big Rapids (Mecosta, MMW)
L.E. KAUFMAN GOLF COURSE, Wyoming (Kent, MMW)
KEARSLEY LAKE GOLF COURSE, Flint (Genesee, MME)
KEEWEENAW MT LODGE, Copper Harbor (Keeweenaw, UP)
KENSINGTON METROPARKS GOLF COURSE, Milford (Oakland)
KIMBERLEY OAKS GOLF CLUB, St Charles (Saginaw, MME)
KINCHELOE MEMORIAL PUBLIC GOLF COURSE, Kinross (Chippewa, UP)
KING PAR GOLF & DRIVING RANGE, Flushing (Genesee, MME)
L'ANSE GOLF CLUB, L'Anse (Baraga, UP)
LAKE CORA HILLS GOLF CLUB, Paw Paw (Van Buren, SW)
LAKE DOSTER GOLF CLUB, Plainwell (Allegan, SW)
LAKE LeANN GOLF COURSE, Somerset Center (Hillsdale, SCen)
LAKE MICHIGAN HILLS GOLF CLUB, Benton Harbor (Berrien, SW)
LAKE MONTEREY GOLF COURSE, Dorr (Allegan, SW)
LAKE O' THE HILLS GOLF COURSE, Haslett (Ingham, SCen)
LAKELAND HILLS GOLF COURSE & LOUNGE, Jackson (Jackson, SCen)
LAKES OF THE NORTH GOLF COURSE, Mancelona (Antrim, NW)
LAKESIDE LINKS GOLF COURSE, Ludington (Mason, NW)
LAKEVIEW HILLS GOLF COURSE, Lexington (Sanilac, MME)
LAKEWOOD ON THE GREEN GOLF COURSE, Cadillac (Wexford, NW)
LAKEWOOD SHORES RESORT, Oscoda (Iosco, NE)
LAPEER COUNTRY CLUB, Lapeer (Lapeer, MME)
LEANING TREE GOLF CLUB, Smiths Creek (St Clair, MSC)
LEDGE MEADOWS GOLF COURSE, Grand Ledge (Eaton, SW)

Alphabetical List of Courses

LES CHENEAUX, Cedarville (Mackinac, UP)
LESLIE PARK GOLF COURSE, Ann Arbor (Washtenaw, WLM)
LIL ACRES GOLF COURSE, Marne (West, grill)
LILAC BROTHERS GOLF COURSE, Newport (Monroe, WLM)
LINCOLN COUNTRY CLUB, Grand Rapids (Kent, MMW)
LINCOLN GOLF CLUB, Muskegon (Muskegon, MMW)
LINCOLN HILLS GOLF COURSE, Birmingham (Oakland)
LINKS AT PINEWOOD GOLF CLUB, Walled Lake (Oakland)
LINKS OF NOVI, Novi (Oakland)
LITTLE TRAVERSE BAY GOLF CLUB, Harbor Springs (Emmet, NW)
LOCH LOMOND GOLF COURSE, Flint (Genesee, MME)
LOWER HURON PAR 3, Belleville (Wayne)
LUM INTERNATIONAL GOLF COURSE, Lum (Lapeer, MME)
MACON GOLF CLUB, Clinton (Lenawee, SCen)
MANISTEE GOLF & COUNTRY CLUB, Manistee (Manistee, NW)
MAPLE HILL GOLF COURSE, Grandville (Kent, MMW)
MAPLE HILLS GOLF CLUB, Augusta (Kalamazoo, SW)
MAPLE LANE GOLF COURSE, Sterling Heights (Macomb, MSC)
MAPLE LEAF GOLF COURSE, Linwood (Bay, MME)
MARION OAKS, Howell (Livingston, WLM)
MARKS GOLF, Lawton (Van Buren, SW)
MARLETTE COUNTRY CLUB, Marlette (Sanilac, MME)
MARQUETTE GOLF & COUNTRY CLUB, Marquette (Marquette, UP)
MARQUETTE TRAILS GOLF COURSE, Baldwin (Lake County, NW)
MARYSVILLE GOLF COURSE, Marysville (St Clair, MSC)
MARYWOOD GOLF CLUB, Battle Creek (Calhoun, SW)
MASON HILLS GOLF CLUB, Mason (Ingham, SCen)
MATHESON GREENS GOLF CLUB, Northport (Leelanau, NW)
MCGUIRE'S GOLF RESORT, Cadillac (Wexford, NW)
MEADOWLANE GOLF COURSE, Kentwood (Kent, MMW)
METRO BEACH GOLF COURSE, Mt Clemens (Macomb, MSC)
MI-RO GOLF COURSE, Douglas (Allegan, SW)
MICHAYWE HILLS GOLF CLUB, Gaylord (Otsego, NE)
MIDDLE CHANNEL COUNTRY CLUB, Harsens Island (St Clair, MSC)
MILHAM PARK GOLF COURSE, Kalamazoo (Kalamazoo, SW)

Jack Berry's Guide to Michigan Golf

MILL CREEK GOLF COURSE, Imlay City (St Clair, MSC)
MILL RACE GOLF COURSE, Jonesville (Hillsdale, SCen)
MISSAUKEE GOLF COURSE, Lake City (Missaukee, NW)
MISSION HILLS GOLF CLUB, Plymouth (Wayne)
MITCHELL CREEK COUNTRY CLUB, Traverse City (Grand Traverse, NW)
MORRISON LAKE COUNTRY CLUB, Saranac (Ionia, MMW)
MOTT PARK GOLF COURSE, Flint (Genesee, MME)
MULBERRY FORE GOLF COURSE, Nashville (Barry, SW)
MULBERRY HILLS COUNTRY CLUB, Oxford (Oakland)
MULLENHURST GOLF COURSE, Delton (Barry, SW)
MULLETT LAKE COUNTRY CLUB, Mullett Lake (Cheboygan, NE)
MUNOSCONG GOLF CLUB, Pickford (Chippewa, UP)
NAHMA, Nahma (Delta, UP)
NEWBERRY COUNTRY CLUB, Newberry (Luce, UP)
NORTH KENT GOLF COURSE, Rockford (Kent, MMW)
NORTH SHORE GOLF CLUB, Menominee (Menominee, UP)
NORTH STAR GOLF COURSE, Ithaca (Gratiot, MMW)
NORTHBROOK GOLF CLUB, Washington (Macomb, MSC)
NORTHWOOD GOLF COURSE, Fremont (Newaygo, MMW)
OAK CREST GOLF COURSE, Norway (Dickinson, UP)
OAK LANE GOLF COURSE, Webberville (Ingham, SCen)
OAK POINTE GOLF CLUB, Brighton (Livingston, WLM)
OAK RIDGE GOLF CLUB, New Haven (Macomb, MSC)
OAK RIDGE GOLF CLUB, Muskegon (Muskegon, MMW)
OAKLAND HILLS GOLF CLUB, Battle Creek (Calhoun, SW)
OAKLAND HILLS GOLF COURSE, Portage (Kalamazoo, SW)
THE OAKS GOLF CLUB, St Joseph (Berrien, SW)
OASIS GOLF CENTER, Plymouth (Wayne)
OCEANA COUNTRY CLUB, Shelby (Oceana, MMW)
OLD CHANNEL TRAIL GOLF COURSE, Montague (Muskegon, MMW)
OLDE MILL GOLF CLUB, Schoolcraft (Kalamazoo, SW)
OLIVET COUNTRY CLUB, Olivet (Eaton, SW)
ONTONAGON GOLF CLUB, Ontonagon (Ontonagon, UP)
ORCHARD HILLS GOLF COURSE, Shelbyville (Allegan, SW)
OT-WELL-EGAN COUNTRY CLUB, Allegan (Allegan, SW)
OVERBROOK, Middleton (Gratiot, MMW)

Alphabetical List of Courses

OXFORD HILLS GOLF & COUNTRY CLUB, Oxford (Oakland)
PALMER PARK GOLF COURSE, Detroit (Wayne)
PARK SHORE GOLF COURSE, Cassopolis (Cass, SW)
PARKVIEW GOLF COURSE, Muskegon (Muskegon, MMW)
PARTRIDGE CREEK GOLF CLUB, Mt Clemens (Macomb, MSC)
PAW PAW LAKE GOLF CLUB, Watervliet (Berrien, SW)
PEBBLE CREEK GOLF CLUB, South Lyon (Oakland)
PEBBLEWOOD GOLF COURSE, Bridgman (Berrien, SW)
PICTURED ROCKS GOLF & COUNTRY CLUB, Munising (Alger, UP)
PIERCE PARK GOLF COURSE, Flint (Genesee, MME)
PINE BROOK GOLF COURSE, Richmond (Macomb, MSC)
PINE CREEK COUNTRY CLUB, Belleville (Wayne)
PINE GROVE COUNTRY CLUB, Iron Mountain (Dickinson, UP)
PINE HILL GOLF CLUB, Brutus (Emmet, NW)
PINE HILLS GOLF COURSE, Laingsburg (Shiawassee, MME)
PINE KNOB GOLF COURSE, Clarkston (Oakland)
PINE LAKES GOLF COURSE, Haslett (Ingham, SCen)
PINE MOUNTAIN GOLF COURSE, Iron Mountain (Dickinson, UP)
PINE RIVER GOLF CLUB, Standish (Arenac, NE)
PINE SHORES GOLF CLUB, St Clair (St Clair, MSC)
PINE TRACE GOLF CLUB, Rochester Hills (Oakland)
PINE VALLEY GOLF CLUB, Romeo (Macomb, MSC)
PINE VIEW GOLF CLUB, Three Rivers (St Joseph, SW)
PINE VIEW GOLF COURSE, Houghton Lake (Roscommon, NE)
THE PINES GOLF COURSE OF LAKE ISABELLA, Weidman (Isabella, MMW)
THE PINES GOLF COURSE, Wyoming (Kent, MMW)
PINEVIEW GOLF COURSE, Ypsilanti (Washtenaw, WLM)
PIPESTONE CREEK, Eau Claire (Berrien, SW)
THE PLAYERS CLUB GOLF COURSE, Lansing (Ingham, SCen)
PLEASANT HILLS GOLF COURSE, Mt Pleasant (Isabella, MMW)
PLEASANT VIEW GOLF COURSE, Saginaw (Saginaw, MME)
PLUM BROOK GOLF CLUB, Sterling Heights (Macomb, MSC)
PLYM PARK GOLF COURSE, Niles (Berrien, SW)
PONTIAC COUNTRY CLUB, Pontiac (Oakland)
PONTIAC MUNICIPAL GOLF COURSE, Pontiac (Oakland)
PORTAGE LAKE GOLF COURSE, Houghton (Houghton, UP)

Jack Berry's Guide to Michigan Golf

PORTLAND COUNTRY CLUB, Portland (Ionia, MMW)
PRAIRIE CREEK GOLF COURSE, DeWitt (Clinton, MMW)
PRAIRIEWOOD GOLF COURSE, Otsego (Allegan, SW)
QUINCY GOLF COURSE, Quincy (Branch, SW)
RACKHAM GOLF COURSE, Huntington Woods (Oakland)
RAISIN RIVER GOLF CLUB, Monroe (Monroe, WLM)
RAISIN VALLEY GOLF CLUB, Tecumseh (Lenawee, SCen)
RAMMLER COUNTRY CLUB, Sterling Heights (Macomb, MSC)
RATTLE RUN GOLF COURSE, St Clair (St Clair, MSC)
RAVENNA GOLF COURSE, Ravenna (Muskegon, MMW)
RED CEDAR GOLF COURSE, Lansing (Ingham, SCen)
RED OAKS GOLF COURSE, Madison Heights (Oakland)
REDDEMAN FARMS GOLF COURSE, Chelsea (Washtenaw, WLM)
RIDGE VIEW GOLF COURSE, Kalamazoo (Kalamazoo, SW)
RIDGEVIEW GOLF CLUB, Belding (Ionia, MMW)
RIVER BEND GOLF COURSE, Hastings (Barry, SW)
RIVER FOREST GOLF COURSE, Flint (Genesee, MME)
RIVERVIEW HIGHLANDS GOLF COURSE, Riverview (Wayne)
RIVERWOOD GOLF CLUB, Mt Pleasant (Isabella, MMW)
ROCHESTER HILLS GOLF & COUNTRY CLUB, Rochester Hills (Oakland)
THE ROCK GOLF COURSE, Drummond Island (Chippewa, UP)
ROGELL GC, Detroit (Wayne)
ROGERS CITY COUNTRY CLUB, Rogers City (Presque Isle, NE)
ROGUE RIVER GOLF COURSE, Sparta (Kent, MMW)
ROLLING HILLS GOLF, Hudsonville (Ottawa, MMW)
ROLLING HILLS GOLF CLUB, Lapeer (Lapeer, MME)
ROLLING HILLS GOLF COURSE, Cass City (Tuscola, MME)
ROLLING HILLS GOLF COURSE, Milan (Washtenaw, WLM)
ROLLING MEADOWS COUNTRY CLUB, Whitmore Lake (Washtenaw, WLM)
ROMEO GOLF COURSE, Romeo (Macomb, MSC)
ROUGE PARK GOLF COURSE, Detroit (Wayne)
ROYAL SCOT GOLF & BOWL, Lansing (Ingham, SCen)
RUSH LAKE HILLS GOLF CLUB, Pinckney (Livingston, WLM)
RUSTIC GLEN GOLF COURSE, Saline (Washtenaw, WLM)
SALEM HILLS GOLF CLUB, Northville (Washtenaw, WLM)
SALT RIVER GOLF COURSE, New Baltimore (Macomb, MSC)

Alphabetical List of Courses

SAN MARINO GOLF COURSE, Farmington Hills (Oakland)
SANDY RIDGE GOLF COURSE, Midland (Midland, MME)
SASKATOON GOLF CLUB, Alto (Kent, MMW)
SAUGANUSH COUNTRY CLUB, Three Rivers (St Joseph, SW)
SAULT STE MARIE COUNTRY CLUB, Sault Ste Marie (Chippewa, UP)
K.I. SAWYER GOLF COURSE, Gwinn (Marquette, UP)
SCENIC GOLF & COUNTRY CLUB, Pigeon (Huron, MME)
SCHUSS MOUNTAIN GOLF CLUB, Mancelona (Antrim, NW)
SCOTT LAKE COUNTRY CLUB, Comstock Park (Kent, MMW)
SHADY HOLLOW GOLF COURSE, Romulus (Wayne)
SHAMROCK HILLS GOLF COURSE, Gobles (Van Buren, SW)
SHANTY CREEK RESORT, Bellaire (Antrim, NW)
SHENANDOAH COUNTRY CLUB, West Bloomfield (Oakland)
SHERWOOD ON THE HILL, Gagetown (Tuscola, MME)
SILVER LAKE GOLF CLUB, Pontiac (Oakland)
SILVER LAKE GOLF COURSE, Brooklyn (Lenawee, SCen)
SOUTH HAVEN GOLF CLUB, South Haven (Allegan, SW)
SOUTHGATE MUNICIPAL GOLF COURSE, Southgate (Wayne)
SOUTHMOOR GOLF COURSE, Burton (Genesee, East)
SPARROW HAWK GOLF COURSE, Jackson (Jackson, SCen)
SPRING BROOK GOLF CLUB, Sterling Heights (Macomb, MSC)
SPRING LAKE GOLF COURSE, Clarkston (Oakland)
SPRING VALLEY, Reed City (Osceola, NW)
SPRING VALLEY GOLF CLUB, Kawkawlin (Bay, MME)
SPRINGBROOK, Springfield (Calhoun, SW)
SPRINGBROOK HILLS GOLF CLUB, Walloon Lake (Charlevoix, NW)
SPRINGDALE GOLF COURSE, Birmingham (Oakland)
SPRINGFIELD OAKS GOLF COURSE, Davisburg (Oakland)
SPRINGPORT HILLS GOLF COURSE, Harrisville (Alcona, NE)
ST. JOE VALLEY GOLF CLUB, Sturgis (St Joseph, SW)
ST. IGNACE, St Ignace (Mackinac, UP)
STATES GOLF COURSE, Ave, Vicksburg (Kalamazoo, SW)
STONEHEDGE GOLF COURSE, Augusta (Kalamazoo, SW)
STONEY CREEK METROPARK, Washington (Oakland)
SUGAR LOAF RESORT, Cedar (Leelanau, NW)

Jack Berry's Guide to Michigan Golf

SUGAR SPRINGS COUNTRY CLUB, Gladwin (Gladwin, NE)
SULTANA PAR 3, Wyandotte (Wayne)
SUMMERGREEN GOLF COURSE, Hudsonville (Ottawa, MMW)
SUNNYBROOK GOLF, BOWLING & MOTEL, Sterling Heights (Macomb)
SWAN VALLEY GOLF COURSE, Saginaw (Saginaw, MME)
SWARTZ CREEK GOLF COURSE, Flint (Genesee, MME)
SYCAMORE GOLF COURSE, Lansing (Ingham, SCen)
SYCAMORE HILLS GOLF CLUB, Mt Clemens (Macomb, MSC)
SYLVAN GLEN GOLF COURSE, Troy (Oakland)
TALL OAKS GOLF COURSE, Romulus (Wayne)
THE TAMARACKS GOLF COURSE, Harrison (Clare, NW)
TANGLEWOOD GOLF CLUB, South Lyon (Oakland)
TAWAS GOLF COURSE, Tawas (Iosco, NE)
TAYLOR MEADOWS GOLF CLUB, Taylor (Wayne)
TEE J'S GOLF COURSE, Mt Clemens (Macomb, MSC)
TERRA VERDE GOLF CLUB, Nunica (Ottawa, MMW)
TERRACE BLUFF COUNTRY CLUB, Gladstone (Delta, UP)
THORNAPPLE CREEK GOLF CLUB, Kalamazoo (Kalamazoo, SW)
THORNE HILLS GOLF COURSE, Carleton (Monroe, WLM)
THUNDER BAY GOLF COURSE, Hillman (Montmorency, NE)
TIMBER RIDGE GOLF COURSE, East Lansing (Ingham, SCen)
TOMAC WOODS GOLF COURSE, Albion (Calhoun, SW)
TORREY PINES GOLF CLUB, Fenton (Genesee, MME)
TREETOPS - SYLVAN RESORT, Gaylord (Otsego, NE)
TURTLE CREEK GOLF CLUB, Burlington (Calhoun, SW)
TWIN BIRCH GOLF COURSE, Kalkaska (Kalkaska, NW)
TWIN BROOKS GOLF CLUB, Chesaning (Saginaw, MME)
TWIN KNOLLS GOLF COURSE, Grass Lake (Jackson, SCen)
TWIN OAKS GOLF COURSE, Freeland (Saginaw, MME)
TWIN OAKS GOLF COURSE, St Johns (Clinton, MMW)
TYLER CREEK GOLF COURSE, Alto (Kent, MMW)
TYRONE HILLS, Fenton (Livingston, WLM)
UNIVERSITY PARK GOLF COURSE, Muskegon (Muskegon, MMW)
VALLEY VIEW FARMS GOLF COURSE, Saginaw (Saginaw, MME)
VALLEY VIEW GOLF CLUB, Shepard (Isabella, MMW)

Alphabetical List of Courses

VASSAR GOLF & COUNTRY CLUB, Vassar (Tuscola, MME)
VERONA HILLS GOLF CLUB, Bad Axe (Huron, MME)
VERONICA VALLEY GOLF COURSE, Lake Leelanau (Leelanau, NW)
VIENNA GREENS GOLF COURSE, Clio (Genesee, MME)
VILLAGE GREEN GOLF CLUB, Newaygo (Newaygo, MMW)
WARFIELD GREENS GOLF CLUB, Fraser (Macomb)
WARREN VALLEY GOLF COURSE, Dearborn Heights (Wayne)
WASHAKIE GOLF & RV RESORT, North Branch (Lapeer, MME)
WATERLOO GOLF COURSE, Grass Lake (Jackson, SCen)
WAVERLY HILLS GOLF COURSE, Lansing (Ingham, SCen)
WAWASHKAMO GOLF CLUB, Mackinac Island (Mackinac, UP)
WAWONOWIN COUNTRY CLUB, Ishpeming (Marquette, UP)
WESBURN GOLF COURSE, South Rockwood (Monroe, WLM)
WEST BRANCH COUNTRY CLUB, West Branch (Ogemaw, NE)
WEST OTTAWA GOLF COURSE, Holland (Ottawa, MMW)
WESTBROOKE GOLF COURSE, Novi (Oakland)
WESTERN GREENS COUNTRY CLUB, Marne (Ottawa, MMW)
WESTLAND MUNICIPAL GOLF COURSE, Westland (Wayne)
WESTSHORE GOLF CLUB, Douglas (Allegan, SW)
WHIFFLETREE HILL GOLF COURSE, Concord (Jackson, SCen)
WHISPERING WILLOWS GOLF CLUB, Livonia (Wayne)
WHITE BIRCH HILLS GOLF COURSE, Bay City (Bay, MME)
WHITE DEER COUNTRY CLUB, Prudenville (Roscommon, NE)
WHITE LAKE OAKS GOLF COURSE, Union Lake (Oakland)
WHITE OAKS GOLF COURSE, Hillsdale (Hillsdale, SCen)
WHITEFISH LAKE GOLF CLUB, Pierson (Montcalm, MMW)
WHITEFORD VALLEY GOLF COURSE, Ottawa Lake (Monroe, WLM)
WICKER HILLS COUNTRY CLUB, Hale (Iosco, NE)
WILDERNESS GOLF COURSE, Carp Lake (Emmet, NW)

WILDERNESS VALLEY GOLF CLUB, Gaylord (Otsego, NE)
WILLOW CREEK GOLF CLUB, Stockbridge (Ingham, SCen)
WILLOW METROPARK GOLF COURSE, New Boston (Wayne)
WILLOW RIDGE GOLF CLUB, Port Huron (St Clair, MSC)
WILLOW SPRINGS GOLF & COUNTRY CLUB, Vassar (Tuscola, MME)
WILLOW TREE GOLF & COUNTRY CLUB, Melvin (Sanilac, MME)
WILLOWBROOK PUBLIC GOLF COURSE, Byron (Genesee, MME)
WINDING CREEK GOLF COURSE, Holland (Allegan, SW)
WINDMILL FARMS RESTAURANT & GOLF COURSE, Mancelona (Antrim, NW)
WINTER GREENS GOLF CLUB, Flushing (Genesee, MME)
WINTERS CREEK GOLF COURSE, Big Rapids (Mecosta, MMW)
WOLVERINE GOLF CLUB & BANQUET CENTER, Mt Clemens (Macomb, MSC)
WOODLAND GOLF CLUB, Brighton (Livingston, WLM)
WOODLAND HILLS GOLF COURSE, Sandusky (Sanilac, MME)
WOODLAWN GOLF CLUB, Adrian (Lenawee, SCen)
WOODSIDE MEADOWS GOLF COURSE, Romulus (Wayne)
WYANDOTTE HILLS GOLF CLUB, Toivola (Houghton, UP)
YANKEE SPRINGS GOLF COURSE, Wayland (Barry, SW)
YE NYNE OLDE HOLLES GOLF CLUB, Charlevoix (Charlevoix, NW)
YE OLDE COUNTRY CLUB, Roscommon (Roscommon, NE)